MASTERS AT WORK

BECOMING A NEUROSURGEON

BECOMING A VETERINARIAN

BECOMING A VENTURE CAPITALIST

BECOMING A HAIRSTYLIST

BECOMING A REAL ESTATE AGENT

BECOMING A MARINE BIOLOGIST

BECOMING AN ETHICAL HACKER

BECOMING A LIFE COACH

BECOMING A YOGA INSTRUCTOR

BECOMING A RESTAURATEUR

BECOMING A PRIVATE INVESTIGATOR

MASTERS AT WORK

BECOMING A NURSE

SONNY KLEINFIELD

SIMON & SCHUSTER

New York   London   Toronto   Sydney   New Delhi

Simon & Schuster
1230 Avenue of the Americas
New York, NY 10020

First Simon & Schuster hardcover edition August 2020

SIMON & SCHUSTER and colophon are registered trademarks
of Simon & Schuster, Inc.

For information about special discounts for bulk purchases,
please contact Simon & Schuster Special Sales at 1-866-506-1949
or business@simonandschuster.com.

The Simon & Schuster Speakers Bureau can bring authors to your
live event. For more information or to book an event, contact
the Simon & Schuster Speakers Bureau at 1-866-248-3049
or visit our website at www.simonspeakers.com.

Manufactured in the United States of America

1   3   5   7   9   10   8   6   4   2

Library of Congress Cataloging-in-Publication Data has been applied for.

ISBN 978-1-9821-4241-4
ISBN 978-1-9821-4242-1 (ebook)

This book was reported and written some months before the COVID-19 outbreak began stealing innocent lives, barricading the world, and testing the capabilities and very soul of the health care system as never before. Nurses are heroes every day. But if there was ever any doubt about their unshakable courage and their indispensable role in fixing the sick, those attributes have been accentuated during every minute of this horrific ordeal. And so this book is dedicated with heartfelt gratitude to all the brave nurses fighting the coronavirus.

CONTENTS

1

He arrived in a wheelchair. Paramedics hustled him in from the ambulance bay, steering him into the sharp light. His face was serious. His eyes jumped left and right, taking in the unfamiliar setting. There was a steadfast procession of such arrivals swerving into the hospital, thickening as the day lengthened. With this man, something was wrong, but it wasn't clear how wrong. All visits to this fast-motion environment were stories with yet unknown endings.

Nurses were coming and going. Doctors were coming and going. Noise was high: the staccato of beeping heart monitors; alarms ringing; phones chirping; the clank of wheeled beds being moved. The grumble and moaning of people and murmurs of misery were catapulting off the walls. And that vivid smell. The pungent disinfectant hospital smell, day in and day out, always the same.

Few places stir up as much drama as rooms like this. Walking in, you feel an electric nervousness that never passes, the nervous flutter of sickness. Patients, with their omnivorous needs, seek its alchemy. The emergency room.

A woman came over to inspect the man in the wheelchair. Her name was Hadassah Lampert. She was thirty-three and a registered nurse, and this was Lenox Hill Hospital, New York City. Every day, Lampert met strangers in pain, and their pain became her concern. Now this man's breathing, his oxygen level, his blood pressure, his heartbeat, the sensation in his face and his limbs, whether he was agreeable or surly, hungry or full, whether, in fact, he lived or died—they were her concern.

He had a trimmed beard on an angular face. Short, dusky hair. Hound dog eyes. Sinewy. He was forty-nine. He wore a baseball cap and had his sunglasses perched on the brim. While she took his vitals, Lampert noticed that he was listing to the left. He told her he had been on the way to work—a blue-collar job—when he felt dizzy and collapsed on the subway.

"Okay, you're going to come over here and lie on the stretcher," she told him.

Helping him transfer over, she noticed that his gait was uneven. She focused hard on him and considered her options. She called a stroke code.

A stroke code was a speeded-up regimen, an auto racing pit stop. A retinue—two nurses, a technician, an ER doctor, a neurologist, a nurse practitioner from neurology, someone from pharmacy—quickly assembled. Lampert economically filled in one of the doctors on the particulars.

The doctor asked the man, "Were you having difficulty walking?"

"Yes."

"What does it feel like?"

"Like things are moving."

The doctor asked him to touch his fingers together.

"Can you go with your finger and touch your nose." A little off.

"Can you touch the tip of your nose?"

"Look at my nose. How many fingers do you see?"

The patient held up two.

"How many fingers?" the doctor asked.

One.

"How many?"

Two.

"What month are we in?"

"September."

"How old are you?"

"Forty-nine."

Lampert escorted him to get a CAT scan of his brain. She and a male nurse hoisted him onto the exam table.

After the table slid into the big doughnut hole, Lampert

and the others positioned themselves around the screen in the control room, the space limited, and stared stonily at the interior of the man's head. No discernable issues. Puzzled looks were swapped. "Weird," the neurologist said, jutting a finger at the image. "This didn't happen overnight. I'm thinking seizure. Maybe he had a tooth issue."

Lampert mentioned that he had had sinusitis, inflamed sinuses. They decided to do an MRI.

While Lampert tended to the man, a young woman awaiting her discharge instructions loped past in her chilly gown, wailing, "I'm telling you, I need to get a life."

In the gathering day, beds were filling up, patients squeezing into the maximized space. A maintenance person was mopping up a dusting of blood from a dripping patient, doing it casually as if cleaning up after a mixer at a reunion, guiding visitors around the freckled area. A "patient experience" volunteer toured the room cradling a highly sociable toy poodle. She whisked it from bed to bed for occupants to pet. "Hi, this is Twitter," she announced. "He weighs three pounds. I put him on a diet if he gains weight." The nurses fussed over him too, appreciating his calming effect.

Among its patchery of cases that morning, the ER had a fall, flank pain, chest pain, suicidal ideation, shortness of breath, rectal bleeding, foreign bodies in the eye, altered medical state, weakness—the various betrayals of the body.

There was a fidgety, caterwauling man who couldn't keep his feet still and glanced over his right shoulder about every nanosecond. At one point, he appeared to be having a conversation with an IV pole. A whimpering woman roughed up by her husband was being interviewed at her bedside by two cops.

The clock on the wall put the time at 9:05 a.m. Lampert's lengthy shift had barely begun.

She accompanied the man to the resuscitation room. A doctor felt his arms. "Do they feel the same?"

"More on the right side."

"If that's one hundred, what is the left side?"

"Sixty or seventy."

Doctor: "There's no stroke. But I think you may be having an infection. Or something going on with your sinuses."

"I was feeling pain in my neck."

The doctor pushed on his neck. "Does this hurt?"

"Yes."

"Did you have any teeth taken out?"

"No."

"You may have had a seizure this morning. Very subtle. So we'll give you some seizure medication. If it improves, that's it."

The attending doctor departed. Lampert saw the troubling-over of the man's eyes and told him, "It's okay, we're going to take care of you. I'm going to give you a medication called Keppra. It's for seizures. If you had a seizure, this will protect you."

The man nodded. He had gone quiet. He was shivering.

"You cold?" Lampert asked.

"Yes."

"We'll get you a blanket."

Lampert turned to a computer terminal near the bed and, clear of mind, began documenting what had been done. She looked over and asked him, "How are you feeling?"

Much of nursing is asking questions. Listening. Looking.

"Tired," he said.

"Well, this medicine makes you a little drowsy. Take a little snooze."

He drank in the scene, one he hadn't anticipated when he rose this morning, this dutiful young woman trying to make him better. He said, "Sorry that I don't speak English that well."

She gave him a warm, open smile. "You speak English beautifully. I have no problem with how you speak English."

Lampert habitually kept these conversations upbeat, which served her well. Emergent nurses are taught about emotional contagion. Getting drawn into the despair of patients makes it harder to do your job. You can catch fear almost like an airborne illness. And if you show it, patients will pick it up.

Project joy and calm and your patients may well absorb those feelings. Nurses chase illness with medicine but they also witness patients who, through cheerfulness, think their way to health.

"Do you smoke?" she asked.

"Yes."

"Every day?"

"I know I should quit. Don't tell my wife."

"We're not going to talk about it now. Right now, we're waiting for the rest of your results to come in. So far, your blood work is good. They're concerned there is some sort of infection. You're going to be admitted. It's annoying to be admitted, but it's the best thing."

"You only have one life."

"Exactly. I like that attitude. We each get one life."

She went out and returned with a cup of water. "I'm going to make sure you can swallow properly. Take a small sip . . . Swallow good . . . Now take a big gulp . . . Swallow . . . Good, you pass."

By 10:15, after considering further results, the doctors re-adjusted their judgment. They believed the man did in fact have a stroke. A stroke can manifest itself either as bleeding in the brain or as a clot. They thought he had a clot. He was now lodged in bed 7, and the plan was to give him a blood thinner. It was called tPA, tissue plasminogen activator. Administered intravenously, it dissolves the clot, improving blood flow to the brain. Time is essential; studies show that if not given within three to four hours, it becomes ineffective. Lampert said, "Time is brain," a common hospital expression for stroke patients, meaning that the sooner a person is treated, the less brain damage they will suffer. (For heart attack patients, the saying goes, "Time is muscle.") The drug can also have the side effect of causing bleeding. Everything in medicine involves risks. The important thing is to weigh the benefits against the risks.

Lampert gave the drug over the course of an hour, keeping vigil at his bedside and checking his vital signs every fifteen minutes. For the first hour, she needed to test his sensation and hand strength. His wife was there now, camped out at the foot of the bed solving word puzzles.

Lampert told him, "This medication is hopefully going to bring your symptoms back. While we give it to you, we're going to be taking your blood pressure very often. We're going to monitor your symptoms. If you have any major change—major headache, major dizziness—you have to tell me."

"Okay."

She took his hands. "Close your eyes and hold your hands out like you're giving a present."

She said, "A little better already."

She told a tech to put him on a portable monitor.

Ritually, she asked him, "You good?"

"Yes."

"We're just hanging out."

A young man appeared with a backpack slung over his shoulder, and Lampert asked, "This your son?"

"Yes."

"You have a great dad," she said to him.

The boy said, "When he wants to be."

With watchful patience, she did a neurological assessment. Ran her hands lightly over the man's cheeks. Over his temples. She had him squeeze her hands. Lift each leg. Raise his hands with his eyes closed.

"Better. Much better. Not a hundred percent, but better."

The treatment continued to reanimate his former self. A little later, as part of the halting steps to full recovery, he was sent upstairs to a room on one of the floors. Lampert went along, telling him, "You're in good hands. You've responded well. I'm so glad." She hugged his wife and son. Her work was finished, the outcome good. Taking a deep breath, she wove her way back to the babble of the ER. You keep moving. Someone else in pain is always waiting.

2

Lampert wore her scrubs—her repetitive work wardrobe of a white top and a royal-blue skirt over matching leggings, sensible black clog-like shoes on her feet—along with the accoutrements of her job. A stethoscope, the most basic piece of medical equipment, extruded from a pocket. Her ID badge dangled from a lanyard draped around her neck. Clipped to the lanyard was a Vocera Badge, a small black plastic device that enabled her to communicate hands-free with anyone in the hospital. A constellation of pins was fastened up and down the lanyard like warrior medals. Most of them are what she calls conversation pieces without relatable meaning. Some held significance. A sepsis pin. A brain pin. Her mother bought her first one for her at the uniform store when she was getting her scrubs. It says, "I ♥ an RN."

Glued onto her plastic badge that read *Registered Nurse* was a sticker headshot of Belle, the book-loving cartoon character from *Beauty and the Beast*. All the time, people tell her she looks like Belle. While she was doing her ER fellowship years ago, a girl patient remarked on the striking resemblance and gave her the sticker. Though it's well worn by now, she doesn't ever want to remove it.

A few years ago, a four-year-old girl having a seizure came to the emergency room. Her parents accompanied her, but she was hysterical. Her name was Madison. Hoping to calm her, her mother said, "Maddy, doesn't the nurse look like Belle?" Indulging this charade, Lampert turned to the girl and said, "Maddy, I'm Belle." This soothed her, she was given a workup, and was sent home in good health. A year later, the mother was admitted to the hospital, nothing too serious. The mother asked one of the other nurses, "Is the nurse who looks like Belle here?" She wanted to reconnect with her, so the nurse located her and Lampert went to the mother's room. She recognized her at once. She told Lampert, "That was so traumatic for Madison, but when we left, the only thing she could talk about was, 'Why wasn't Belle wearing her dress?' And I told her, 'Well, she can't wear it while she's at work.'" Madison was only in kindergarten, but she told her mother that she wanted to become a nurse.

Lampert has been a nurse for almost ten years. She has dark hair that sweeps down her back; a round, alert face; and an incandescent smile. Colleagues and supervisors applaud the precision of her nursing skills and addictive charm. Nursing is hard work that takes imagination and depth of feeling, and those who work with Lampert single out her reserves of compassion and empathy, how she genuinely cares for her patients. Some of them call her a "rock star."

As always, she walked briskly, moving with a certain authority, and hit almost every hand sanitizer she passed. Nurses wash their hands dozens, if not hundreds, of times a day. No one has cleaner hands than nurses. She picked up a new patient. A twenty-seven-year-old man with a rock-ribbed face. He had dropped by the hospital to look in on his mother, who had undergone a procedure upstairs. Now he was lying on one of the sturdy hospital beds in the emergency room.

"How do you feel now?" Lampert asked him.

"Embarrassed. Extremely embarrassed." His mouth had gone dry and he had trouble getting the words out. He had a look of confusion on his face.

His mother's procedure had gone fine. It was mentioned that there had been some bleeding. He heard that word. He grew dizzy. As he was walking down the corridor, his head began to spin. Suddenly he passed out, striking his head on the vinyl floor.

"That happens," Lampert said. "But we'll see that you're all right."

His father stood next to him and said with an abashed smile, "He doesn't like blood or even hearing the word 'blood.'"

Wrinkling his nose, he rounded off his thought: "I'm telling you, he just hears that word 'blood' and he goes blotto."

"Well, that settles one thing," Lampert said. "He's not going to be a nurse."

Over the years, I've known a fair number of nurses—nurses in their professional capacity when I've been an agitated patient, as well as nurses who were friends. I've always admired them, both for what it is they do and for how they do it. The whole idea of nursing impresses me: its quiet heroism, how nurses show what kindness looks like and can remake your notion of goodness. They work in a self-contained universe of pain and sadness with poise, yet too often, I've felt nurses are undersung and misunderstood. Healed people leave the hospital and rave about the marvels of what doctors did to repair them, rarely giving deserved mention to the conscientious nurses, so often their guides to recuperation.

Nurses form the intersection between patient and doctor, the entry point into medical care. They see horrors most people can't imagine, and many we prefer not to think about. What others find unpleasant, they find normal. They see people at their weakest, most desperate moments, but are not discomfited by the uncomfortable. There's nothing easy about being a nurse, but where would we be without them? They help us live and die. They hold our lives in their hands.

Nurses are the largest profession in health care. Roughly

four million nurses are at work in the United States. That means one in eighty people is a nurse. It's a stratified profession, involving a hierarchy of empowerment. Some three million are registered nurses, according to the U.S. Department of Labor, by far the largest category. When someone mentions that they're a nurse, they usually mean they're an RN. When you say *nurse*, that's what people think of. There are also some 730,000 licensed practical nurses and about 250,000 advanced practice registered nurses.

What a nurse is allowed to do is dictated by each state's Nurse Practice Act and is governed by a state board of nursing. RNs fully oversee a patient's recovery. They administer medication, perform tests, draw blood, insert catheters, answer questions, interpret test results, and emotionally boost the spirits of the bodies in their care. To qualify as an RN, you typically need to either obtain an associate's degree in nursing (ADN) or a bachelor of science in nursing (BSN). Then it's necessary to pass the National Council Licensure Examination for registered nurses.

Licensed practical nurses (LPNs) are more restricted. Working under the supervision of an RN or doctor, they perform basic care like assisting with dressings, taking vital signs, doing vaccinations, assembling equipment, and transferring patients. They also get involved in updating medical records and billing. An LPN must complete an educational program that normally takes a year, and then obtain a license.

There are also advanced practice registered nurses (APRN), most of whom are nurse practitioners. They are an elevated class, closer to doctors, and can serve as a person's primary care provider, diagnosing and prescribing medications. There are also clinical nurse specialists, certified nurse-midwives, and certified registered nurse anesthetists. To reach these levels of nursing requires a master's degree or doctorate.

Nothing about nursing is monolithic. There are probably over a hundred varieties of nursing jobs. There are pediatric nurses and geriatric nurses and women's health nurses. There are doctor's office nurses and legal nurse consultants and hospice nurses. School nurses and military nurses and cruise ship nurses. Emergency room nurses and intensive care nurses and operating room nurses. Radiology nurses and oncology nurses and post-anesthesia nurses. Home health care nurses and nurse case managers and forensic nurses. Public health nurses and burn care nurses and rehabilitation nurses. Camp nurses and telephonic triage nurses and bioterrorism nurses. There are nurse informaticists, who analyze data and implement the systems that other nurses depend on. There are travel nurses who work for agencies who dispatch them to interim assignments around the country—three months in Florida, three months in Hawaii, three months in South

Dakota—to fill in at short-staffed medical facilities. There are flight transport nurses and HIV/AIDS nurses and prison nurses. There are nurses who only teach and nurses who rise to hospital management positions. By far, the largest employers of RNs are hospitals; they're where you find more than 60 percent of all nurses.

People have great faith in nurses. Gallup surveys for eighteen consecutive years have voted them the most trusted professionals, with some 85 percent of respondents listing them first in honesty and ethics, well ahead of teachers, doctors, and pharmacists (car salesmen and members of Congress tend to limp in last). Since 1999, when Gallup first started inquiring about this matter, nurses have led in all but one year: 2001, the year of the 9/11 attacks. Firefighters rose to the top.

3

Lenox Hill Hospital, a grouping of ten functionalist buildings, sprawls across a full block on the Upper East Side of Manhattan, bounded by East Seventy-Sixth and Seventy-Seventh Streets, and Park and Lexington Avenues. It's a pleasant, high-energy area. Cars clog the streets, moving at a sludgy pace. Shoals of pedestrians are always sliding by, many of them tugged by bouncy dogs. Sirens seem to go off every couple of minutes, the emblematic voices of hurrying fire trucks and cop cars and ambulances. As this pushing procession of humanity flows along Seventy-Seventh Street, it seems as if every tenth or twentieth person halts and turns into Lenox Hill Hospital.

The hospital was founded in 1857 to care for immigrants. Originally, its name was the German Dispensary and it was located downtown on Canal Street. Beginning in 1868, it gradually moved uptown and eventually changed its name to match its host neighborhood. Today, it is part of the Northwell Health System, boasts four hundred and fifty beds, and serves some hundred and sixty thousand patients a year. Over the years, patients have included Winston Churchill (struck by a car while crossing the street nearby), Elizabeth Taylor, Pat Nixon, James Cagney, Brooke Astor, and Rocky Graziano. Lady Gaga was born here.

In area, the ER at Lenox Hill is 14,300 square feet, roughly a quarter the size of a football field, and is the gateway to the hospital. In capacity, it can handle sixty or seventy patients at a time, and often does. "The most I've ever seen was eighty, which is insane for a space this size," Lampert said. It isn't possible to turn a sign on the door saying: *CLOSED. COME BACK LATER*. The iron law of the ER is it can't refuse walk-ins, yet if it runs out of beds to treat critical care patients—something that happens not even once a year—it can ask the EMS system to divert ambulances elsewhere temporarily. On an average weekday, the ER treats approximately a hundred and sixty to a hundred and eighty patients, slowing to a hundred and thirty on weekends. Mondays are busiest. Even sick people don't necessarily want to rearrange their weekend plans, so, mangling the definition of an emergency, they stop by on Monday at their convenience. For all of 2018, the ER handled fifty-six thousand patients. This is where I came, shift after shift, to watch Hadassah Lampert do the business of nursing.

The ER is bisected between the north and south sides,

and follows a "split-flow" process. The south side keeps more store-like hours, open eight a.m. to midnight, and treats milder cases. The north side addresses serious cases and, like a casino, never closes. Time is irrelevant. Lampert almost always works the north side. The south side looks different. Known as the "treat and release" portion, it expects its patients won't be admitted to the hospital. Arrivals sit in fat cushioned chairs rather than lie supine on beds, as they do in the north. Studies indicate that once you place someone on a stretcher, that lengthens their stay in the ER by at least an hour. "It's psychological," Lampert told me. "People lie down and they get too comfortable. They settle in. They don't want to move. People who are twenty years old suddenly need to use a bedpan. A lot of times people come to the ER and they become infantile and want everything done for them." To avoid that slippery slope toward sedentariness, the nurses keep patients who inhabit the south side vertical. A wise veteran cardiologist at Lenox Hill always reminds colleagues, "Stay vertical."

Ringing the exterior of the north side are twenty numbered spaces, referred to as beds, though in fact two beds fill each space. They are curtained off to afford a modicum of privacy. The squished-in beds are such that neighboring patients can reach out and clutch hands, the spaces seemingly too small for the important activity that takes place within them. Ad-

ditional beds lie in several rooms with actual doors. Two are
negative-pressure rooms, where air only flows inward, in the
event someone arrives with a contagious, airborne disease.
Another room is for children, and one is for patients who
might need a bathroom constantly or have migraines and require quiet. In one corner is a resuscitation room with two
beds for patients requiring urgent care. Cabinets with pull-
out trays contain things like rapid infusion tubing, central
lines, GlideScope blades, waveform capnography disposable
thoracotomy trays, full-body warming blankets. The ER also
has its own radiology suite, equipped with a CAT scanner
and two X-ray machines, along with a portable version for
use at bedside.

The beds fill up quickly. After patients get discharged,
crumpled sheets are yanked off, the beds remade and their
transient successors are lying there, the activity like tables
being turned over in a well-reviewed restaurant. Once all
spots are claimed, patients are shoehorned into every con-
ceivable square foot, flagrantly laid out in the center of the
room or shoved against the walls in the corridors. You hear
reactions like, "Christ, I'm ninety-two years old and they put
me in the hall." The morning tends to be slow, the ER usually inheriting less than ten patients from the night shift. By
noon, the census often rises to thirty, building to maybe fifty
by three in the afternoon. There could be seventy by five, the

place up-tempo and choked with people. Finally, the ER begins to thin out into the evening and overnight. The stream of people, though, basically never ceases.

The north side is divided into two zones, and, at full staff, four nurses work each zone. Zone One is beds 14–20; Zone Two is beds 1–7. Beds 8 to 13 are holding beds for admitted patients awaiting available rooms upstairs.

In the center of the ER is a nurses' station, drenched in fluorescent light, with work areas and wheeled chairs where nurses, doctors, managers, and clerks bunch together. This serves as the nerve center. A charge nurse, who runs the flow of the ER, positions herself in the left-hand corner. In easy eyesight are a computer screen showing the active patients and their status, as well as another displaying the heart monitors in each bed, the jiggling lines and digits of life.

A plaque adorning one wall of the ER is incised with the department's HEROES AT THE HILL, attesting to the month's four exceptional employees. An inscription proclaims: NOT ALL HEROES WEAR CAPES. SOME JUST WEAR SCRUBS. Elsewhere hang bulletin boards with thumbtacked homage from discharged patients:

> *"A nurse very tall with a deep voice and a bald head was extremely nice and very passionate."*

A nurse "put my phone in a charger for me. I know it sounds small, but I really appreciated it."

". . . did a first-class, pain-free job of stapling my scalp."

As at other hospitals, patient experience surveys are given out, the results reviewed monthly. These days, patients also funnel their opinions to Yelp and other internet destinations. Along with their judgments on restaurants and mold cleaners, they'll post how their muscle cramp was treated at the ER.

More formally, the Joint Commission, which accredits hospitals, performs a survey every three years, and the State Department of Health does random checks as well.

The ER is the nurses' environment, and they control it. Nurses manage the churn, assign levels of acuity to patients, and spend the most time ministering to them. Throughout the day, the place vividly expresses what Lampert considers organized chaos. People drift in with everything that can go wrong with the human body, in a graphic daily montage. Heart attack. Stroke. Broken tibia. Migraine. Aneurysm. Pneumonia. Abscess. Ulcer. Kidney stone. Contusion. Constipation. Depression. Burns. Dislocated shoulder. Hiatal hernia. Crick in the neck. Appendicitis. Pre-eclampsia. Laceration. Dog bite. Rat bite. Back pain. Stomach pain. Arm pain. Leg pain. Head pain. Tooth pain. Referred shoulder pain. Throat pain. Right rib pain. Enigmatic pain. Up and down the severity ladder of human distress, including conditions that are not in the faintest sense an emergency, condensed together and brought to this space. It is necessary to make room for surprises.

"Just when you say you've seen everything, then you see something you haven't seen before," says Cathy Fogarty, Lenox Hill's big-hearted director of patient services who oversees the nurses in the ER. "And then the next day you'll see something else you've never seen before."

Lenox Hill is not designated a trauma center, so it rarely sees stabbings, car accident injuries, or gunshot wounds, unless they happen right outside its doors. One doctor did mention he had treated a guy shot by a BB gun. But it regularly gets falls and other traumas, in which case it is expected to stabilize the patient before sending them to a trauma hospital. Lenox Hill sits above the number 6 subway line. People hit by trains have been wheeled upstairs and into the ER.

In this tight world of high stress, the nurses fill many roles, doing everything from assessing and monitoring arriving patients, drawing blood and giving medications, to changing sheets and emptying bedpans. The ER employs patient care techs, who assist nurses by handling quotidian tasks like taking vitals and dealing with bedpans and bathing patients.

"We'd be nowhere without them," Lampert said. "They're invaluable." But nurses still perform those things during busy hours. You don't let your patient sit on a bedpan because the techs are unavailable.

Nurses also explain discharge instructions to patients, and answer questions about what is being done to them in understandable language. Some patients simply want to talk and have someone listen. Cheerfully, nurses listen. Patients are much sicker than they used to be and are living longer, taking more from a nurse.

Doctors issue the orders that nurses carry out, but nurses use their own judgment, questioning instructions that seem inappropriate or wrong. Experience matters. Nurses witness the identical problems again and again in different bodies, and instinctively know what to do. But also, there are inevitable mysteries that reveal themselves in glimpses.

"We solve puzzles here in the ER," Fogarty told me. "We're detectives in scrubs."

4

The first thing Lampert did when she arrived in the rising morning was stash her belongings in the break room. Then she attended the stand-up huddle meeting. That's when ER issues get aired and the weary night shift nurses fill in the incoming day shift on what happened on their watch, a cataloging of the state of the ER. Nurses hand off the patients they had intimately cared for to their replacements. A normal day in the ER begins with eight nurses, an ensemble that builds to sixteen by afternoon, then shrinks back to eight at night.

Huddle meetings go quickly, typically consuming only a few minutes. Without preamble, the nurse manager did a recap: "We have six patients. It was crazy last night, but we're okay now." Among them was a man assigned a one-to-one—designated for suicidal patients or someone hallucinating—when a tech had to sit within arm's reach at all times. Two were serious cases admitted to the hospital but awaiting beds upstairs.

All in all, the place might be described as "quiet," except that's a word taboo among nurses. The unwritten rules forbade verbalizing the level of inactivity. The ER could be practically unpeopled, but don't say it's quiet. That will surely jinx things and the ER will be mobbed. One time I made the mistake of asking a nurse, "Is it quiet today?" and she stared at me in horror and snapped, "I don't answer that question." She told Lampert, and she shook her head and said solemnly, "Never ask that." Lampert also confirmed for me the power of full moons, how their appearance somehow starts a stampede to the front doors of the ER.

The nurse manager gave a protocol update: "If a patient comes in with a port already accessed, we have to reaccess it. If there's an infection and we don't reaccess it, we own the infection. Remember, we don't know what patients are doing before they get here. We had a patient take Ativan on his own from his own stash."

She read off who would go where. Who to each zone, who to the south side, who was the front triage nurse who classified walk-in patients, who was the ambulance triage nurse, and who was the charge nurse. The assignments changed every shift. Today, Lampert was doing front triage for two hours, then switching to Zone One.

As is true at most hospitals, the nurses worked twelve-hour shifts, three days a week, thirteen shifts a month. The main shifts stretch from eight a.m. to eight p.m., then eight p.m. to eight a.m., with some nurses working swing shifts from ten a.m. to ten p.m. and others from noon to midnight. Lampert works the main day shift. She gets a forty-five-minute break in the morning and an hour in the evening. Her work days vary, though she's able to map out a schedule for the upcoming two months. Right now, she was doing two shifts a week, because she was enrolled in a doctorate program to become a nurse practitioner. It's a career path that many ambitious nurses pursue.

Twelve-hour shifts became common starting in the 1980s. They were thought to provide more continuity of care than if nurses worked eight hours and made three shift changes a day, though that value is debatable. Nurses, however, generally welcome getting four days a week off. Many of them take on per diem jobs at other medical facilities to add to their income. Some studies question the wisdom of such long hours, finding that they chip away at the brain and contribute to errors. Nurses are always talking about how tired they are. Lampert told me, "I like them. It's nice once you're in the motion of work to stay another four hours and then have four days off."

Rain splashed down outside as Lampert parked herself at the triage desk, set behind glass just inside the entrance and away from the mumble of the ER. A dozen patients clustered in the waiting area, kept occupied by thumbing through magazines or staring stoically at breaking-news updates un-spooling on a TV mounted on the wall. One woman was knitting a sweater. Another drenched in too much perfume had shown up with her hair in rollers. A wizened man was declaring into his phone: "No, I'm not at Macy's. I'm at the emergency room."

Taped to the window frame in front of Lampert were rel-evant reminders: What to look for with measles. The signs of a stroke. Dizziness—pertinent questions.

Doing triage, you can't help but think that everyone on earth is sick, that being sick is normal. Lampert has precise thoughts about how to approach the work. "The triage nurse is the first person you see," she told me. "How you say the first thing to them matters. Do you start out, 'Why are you here today?' or do you say, 'Hi, I'm Hadassah, what's going on, sorry we have to meet in this way.' It takes the same amount of time and effort. But you're setting a different mood."

No one does triage all shift. The limit is six hours. Dr. Yves Duroseau, the head of the Emergency Department, told me: "You're being bombarded with terrible stories. A kid falls off the monkey bars. The nanny brings him in. The parents are hysterical. A person brings in Grandpa, who's at the end of life and has one leg off this earth, and they want every-thing done. And everything in between. It's too intensive a shift to do for that long."

When I asked Lampert about it, she said, "It's stressful. It's annoying, too, to be honest. Listening to that many patients, constantly talking people off the cliff."

The hospital's goal is to move patients, on average, from the door to a doctor within thirty minutes, which it says it regularly meets, and to treat and release them within three hours (a goal not yet attained). Whenever a nurse feels an imperiled patient needs quick attention, she can call an "upgrade." Then a doctor reports to the patient at once.

Lampert and the other emergency room nurses are taught the Emergency Severity Index scale, created by two American emergency room doctors. It's a method to synthesize flickers of information and rapidly sort patients by assigning a degree of acuity from level 1 (most serious) to level 5 (nonurgent). The sorting says who needs to be seen quickly, and who can safely linger behind more serious patients. If Lampert assigns a patient too low a level, that puts them at risk. If too high, resources will be kept from someone in more pressing need.

The decisions are anchored in telltale evidence like what the patient says, past medical history, age, vital signs, and what the nurse notices (Is the person writhing? Is their face pale? Are they favoring one side?) and, with less serious cases, how many "resources" like blood work and X-rays the nurse expects will be needed. Five vital signs are read and evaluated: blood pressure, temperature, oxygen level, respiration rate, and pulse. A level 1, for instance, could be someone in cardiac arrest or suffering massive bleeding. Level 2 could be chest pain or an asthma attack. A level 3 might be stomach pain or a high fever. Level 4 might be a laceration. Level 5 could be a splinter in the big toe or someone who needs an Alka-Seltzer and a glass of water.

Nurses can be fooled. Kids tend to be particularly befuddling; they often will deceive you right up to the last minute. Young and healthy, they offer smudged accounts, generally don't look nearly as ill as they actually are.

Lampert lifted her gaze from the computer terminal and scanned the waiting room. "Oddly enough, sometimes the sickest patients of all come in here not by ambulance," she said. "Either they walk in for the silliest things, or they're really sick but manage to get in on their own."

"What are the silliest things?" I asked her.

"Pain for six months and they come in today," she said. "Pain for six years and they come in today. Or a bug bite. Or they need a refill for their medication."

"Really?" I said.

"Really."

The mad logic of the ER. Some people limp in looking death in the face. Others come because they had a bad dream about a duck or were having a boring day.

Lampert called a name over the loudspeaker. Arriving

through the door was a septuagenarian with a thatch of bristly hair, who settled in a chair next to Lampert, twisting one foot behind the other. She kept glancing from side to side, as if on guard against assailants.

"Hi, I'm Hadassah, I'm a nurse here," Lampert said. "What is your problem?"

"Pain."

"Where's the pain?"

"I'm having a lot of pelvic pain. I had an ovary removed and I haven't been taking good care of myself, and the pain is getting worse."

"When was it worst?"

"Two weeks ago."

The woman's face loosened and she began to cry. "I'm having trouble sitting. I took the wrong train. It took me a while to get here."

"Okay, you're here now," Lampert said. "We're going to take care of you. If you had to rate your pain from zero to ten, ten being the worst and zero being no pain at all, where would it be?"

"I feel ten. I don't know."

"That's okay. Ten is ten."

"I'm scared," the woman said. "I think it's something really wrong."

"Don't jump the gun. We'll take care of you."

Lampert rated her level 3 and had her escorted inside.

Next, a sixty-eight-year-old woman with two black eyes, cuts on her forehead, face trampled by pain. It looked like she had been at the bad end of a mixed martial arts match. She was mashing a handkerchief in her hand.

"Hello, I'm Hadassah, come sit."

After the woman recounted the facts of her case, Lampert summed up the diaristic account back to her: "So, you felt dizzy and fell down the steps yesterday morning. You thought you would be okay and put ice on it. Then you woke up and you were like this and had a headache."

"Yes."

Lampert called the charge nurse to tell her she wanted to upgrade the woman. "I feel like it's the safe thing to do," she said. Level 2.

"Feel better," Lampert said, her customary parting remark.

In. Out. They kept coming, in unceasing numbers, people transfigured by pain. Sick to sicker to less sick. Toe pain. Stomach pain. Jaw pain. Questions about their cramped accounts answered in bitten-off sentences. Yes. No. Not really. With each patient, Lampert attached a white wrist band bearing a bar code and name and birth date. Additional wristbands were clipped on as called for: red for allergy, yellow for fall risk, pink for do not use extremity (for blood draws or to check blood pressure), blue for critical airway.

Next, a heavy-shouldered man with a halo of steel-gray hair complained in a twangy accent of pain in the back of his head. His eyes were glued to the ceiling as if studying constellations. "It's been increasing the last two weeks and I'm having trouble sleeping," he said. "When I lie down and try to sleep, it's like a mission."

"I googled it," he went on. "Google told me I have diabetes. I have HIV."

Lampert laughed and put her eyebrows up. "Well, Google did not go to school."

"My relative who goes to college in Florida, she said, do not google it."

"That's right, don't google it."

"It told me I might be having a stroke."

"No," Lampert said.

She asked, "If you had to rate your pain, one to ten with ten being the worst, what would you rate it?"

He removed a piece of gum from his mouth and rolled it between his fingers, while saying, "It's now like a five. At night, it's like nine or ten. It feels like it's literally trying to come out the back of my head."

Her calibration: level 4.

Elderly woman. Assertive eyes. Cropped hair. Quizzical look.

"Hello, I'm Hadassah, how are you?"

"Well, fine."

"You're fine, but you're here. So you can't be that fine. What's going on?"

"I have abdominal pain when I take some medication."

"What's your pain level?"

"Now it's not so bad."

"Maybe one, two?"

"Maybe three, four."

Two seconds passed.

"Well, to be safe, make it six."

Summoned in next was a slope-chinned guy with a stringy body, wearing a T-shirt with the legend worn away. He was here several days before and suspected of insurance fraud.

"Hello, sir, I just saw you last week."

Looking level-browed at her, he said, "You didn't see me. You saw my brother."

"Your brother. Okay, what's going on?"

"I think I have an abscess in my mouth. And I don't want to fight today. I just put my dad in the hospital."

He went inside, to see a doctor and a hospital official who would have some questions that might add to his pain.

During a lapse, Lampert spoke to me about the assessments. "Once you're above level 4, it's how sick they are. Four or 5, it's more how many resources are going to be used. Anyone over forty with chest pain would automatically be a level 2. You have to rule out cardiac arrest. The levels can change. Someone comes in and they fell. They're level 4. You X-ray them and there are six broken ribs. They would have been level 2."

By dint of her experience, Lampert can complete these accordioned evaluations in a few minutes, through just brisk ribbons of conversation. "You can't spend more time than that or this ER can blow up," she said. "We don't want to keep people waiting. Some places, like at the city hospitals, you can wait five hours in the ER. We don't do that."

Lampert is single and lives in Rockland County, a suburb north of the city. It suits her. "It's so peaceful there. At night, you don't hear anything. Just crickets." She drives to work. In the mornings, when she blends into the start of the morning rush, it takes her about an hour and ten minutes. Going home back to the rest of her life, evening shading into night, she makes it in forty-five minutes.

She was working toward her doctorate at Rutgers University in Newark, New Jersey, a less calm environment. "I heard on the radio today that there were eight shootings in Newark in the last two weeks," she said. "And they said that was an improvement." She was specializing in emergency medicine and family medicine. "For my doctorate I want to examine bounce backs, why patients return to the ER in a few days for the same thing," she said. "I think it's often they didn't understand the discharge instructions. Either they didn't follow the discharge instructions or they didn't get a follow-up with their doctor or they didn't fill a prescription. Another problem is Google. People google and self-diagnose and don't trust the evidence."

The next patient was an animated woman, here for a PICC line placement to deliver antibiotics at home—takeout medicine—to resolve an infection. After she sank into the chair, Lampert told her she needed to check if the woman was at the correct place. Staring right at her, the woman told her, "You've got an attitude."

Lampert overlooked the woman's remark and repeated, "I need to be sure you are where you should be. It will just take a moment."

The woman said, "I was supposed to come to the hospital yesterday and get it."

"So why didn't you come yesterday?"

The woman snapped, "I had a houseful of grandchildren. What, you want me to bring a houseful of grandchildren here? So that's what you want?"

"I was just asking."

Level 3, with an attitude of level 1.

Young man in jeans and sweatshirt, a tattoo of a watch on his right wrist.

"Hi, I'm Hadassah, what's going on?"

"I'm in bad shape right here. I don't do doctors or nothing, but I'm in bad shape." Coughing, he itched his head.

"You don't do doctors," Lampert said, making conversation. "Well, it's a good thing I'm a nurse, then. So, what happened?"

"I woke up this morning and started brushing my teeth and I started throwing up blood. I got on the subway and I could taste blood in my mouth."

"Any fevers, chills?"

"Yes, chills. I'm freezing and sweating."

"This morning."

"Every morning."

"For how long?"

"Couple of weeks."

Vomiting, level 3.

"Feel better."

Next patient. A scrubbed man in his early forties, a regal bearing. Mirthful eyes. His complaint was that he was having pain when swallowing. Itchy throat. His doctor told him to take a Benadryl and go to the ER, so here he was. Lampert asked him to open his mouth and she took a look. Level 3.

Disconsolate man with tufty eyebrows accompanied by his wife and child in a stroller. His back was killing him. Started this morning. Speaking with animation, he said, "I drove to Philly yesterday and helped someone move. I felt it yesterday.

It wasn't bad. This morning, I couldn't get out of bed. It was real bad, like monster bad."

"If you had to give your pain a number, zero to ten, ten is the worst and zero is nothing, what would it be?"

"I'd say eight. But, you know, I don't know if it's pain. It's more like unusual discomfort. Or like a real bad annoyance."

"Everyone has their own version of what pain is."

"Okay, then put me down at version eight."

Noted and processed. Level 4.

Lampert said, "Feel better."

5

From the dawn of time, women and sometimes men cared for the ill in their tribes in a manner that could be considered nursing. Wet nurses paid to breastfeed the babies of mothers are mentioned in ancient writings. King Tut, in fact, built a tomb to honor Maia, his wet nurse. Such antecedents are why some consider it the oldest profession. There is evidence of nurses in Roman times. In Romans 16:1, the Apostle Paul refers to Phoebe, a Christian deaconess, as conceivably the first visiting nurse. Knights sent by Pope Urban II to fight during the Crusades became nurses to the wounded. The field was not always honorable. In early modern Europe, it was done ad hoc by old, uneducated women. Some were drunk. Some stole. Some heinously extorted money from their patients.

Nursing as a skilled profession, though, owes its existence to a single woman: Florence Nightingale. She is by far the most famous nurse in the profession's history. Born in Florence, Italy, in 1820 to a wealthy British family, she felt motivated to help the poor and ill in the English village where her family occupied a lavish estate. She concluded that nursing was God's plan for her. Her parents, however, frowned on the idea, viewing nursing as menial work that was beneath her, and wouldn't allow her to obtain any training. Determined to follow through on her desires, she figured it out on her own and enrolled as a nursing student at a school in Germany.

When she returned to London, she got a job as a nurse in a hospital for sick governesses. During the Crimean War in 1853, she was recruited by the secretary of war to assemble a team of fellow nurses to minister to the wounded at Scutari, the understaffed British base hospital in Crimea. The fallen soldiers were badly neglected and conditions were horrendous. The hospital sat above an actual cesspool. Rodents infested the place. Soldiers wasted away in their own excrement. Nightingale was instrumental in improving the conditions and she saved many lives. She worked indefatigably, barely reserving any time to sleep. Circling through the dark hallways in the evenings while carrying a lamp, she acquired her legendary nickname, "the Lady with the Lamp." When she returned to England, she was welcomed as a hero.

She saw firsthand the clear need for more sophisticated training for nurses, which would allow them to flourish in their occupation. She wrote a great deal about health care and brought on sorely needed reform. In 1859, she published a brief book, *Notes on Nursing: What It Is, and What It Is Not.* It remains remarkably relevant—stressing the need for pure air, light, and cleanliness for the sick, and the importance of sound observation in nursing. Tips like: "Come back and look at your patient *after* he has had an hour's animated conversation with you. It is the best test of his real state." And: "Let your doubt be to yourself, your decision to them." In 1860, Nightingale went on to establish the St. Thomas' Hospital, along with the Nightingale Home and Training School for Nurses in London. Afterward, many nursing schools opened worldwide. Writers hailed Nightingale's greatness in songs, plays, and poems. Girls wanted to grow up to be her. Nursing came to be looked on as an enviable profession. All nurses working today owe a significant debt of gratitude to Florence Nightingale.

While she was at Scutari, Nightingale contracted a bacterial infection known as Crimean Fever. It steadily took its toll on her. By the time she was thirty-eight, she was essentially bedridden in her home. Undeterred by her illness, she continued to advocate for health care reform from her bed through her writings, which set the foundation for modern professional nursing. She lived to be ninety.

Another giant of nursing was Clara Barton. She was born in 1821 in Oxford, Massachusetts, where her father was a well-to-do farmer. She was an extremely bashful child who dreaded social interactions. Yet she found something in helping others. When her brother fell off a barn roof and suffered a serious head injury, she took it upon herself to care for him, acquiring a taste for nursing. Doctors felt he wouldn't make it. Barton dismissed such forecasts. She learned how to administer medicine. She placed leeches on her brother to bleed him. He recovered fully.

True story: to settle on her career path, her family asked a famous phrenologist, L. N. Fowler, to examine her and offer a verdict. After scrupulously measuring the bumps on her head, he advised her to become a teacher. She did. She even founded the first free school in New Jersey. However, she quit teaching upon discovering to her disgruntlement that a man had been hired at a salary twice hers. She moved to Washington and found work as a recording clerk in the U.S. Patent Office.

When the Civil War broke out in 1861, Barton wanted to be involved. At first, she distributed supplies to the Union Army, then worked as an independent nurse. She had had no formal medical training, because precious little was available for nurses. She managed as a self-taught nurse. Week after week, she cared for soldiers at every major battlefield: Fredericksburg, Antietam. Time and again, she found herself in grave danger. In her closest call, an enemy bullet ripped through the sleeve of her blouse before killing the soldier she was nursing. She came to be known as the "Angel of the Battlefield" as well as the "Florence Nightingale of America."

After the war, she wrote and lectured extensively about her experiences. While traveling through Europe in 1870, she worked during the Franco-Prussian War with the disaster relief organization known as the International Red Cross, based in Geneva. When she returned to the U.S., she pushed for the establishment of an American version. Due to her efforts, the American Red Cross was founded in 1881. Barton was its first president. She worked for no salary. Discontent over her autocratic leadership led to her being forced out in 1904, when she was eighty-three. Later, she founded the National First Aid Society. She died in 1912.

Up until the late 1800s, nurses in the U.S. primarily learned to become nurses empirically, by working as apprentices to experienced nurses. There were, as well, scattered training lectures given by doctors. The epic need for nurses to care for the wounded during the Civil War hastened a burst of nursing schools. In 1873, the first true ones opened: the New York Training School at Bellevue Hospital in New York, the Connecticut Training School at the State Hospital, and the Boston Training School at Massachusetts General Hospital. Based on the principles of Florence Nightingale, they were known as the Nightingale schools. Nowadays, thousands of nursing programs exist and around a thousand schools offer bachelor's degrees in nursing.

6

There are many unexpected heights to nursing, indelible and even miraculous moments that remain with nurses. These moments nourish them and ground them. They become the story they tell about their profession, and nurses like to tell stories. One clammy afternoon when Lampert was off from work, I met her in a warmly decorated hotel lobby in midtown. Compared to the ER, it was library-quiet. She had attended a nursing conference and was bent over her laptop. In a ruminative mood when I inquired about memorable nursing experiences, she told me this one:

"It was my first patient coming off orientation, my first night shift on my own. I was in the urology unit. This woman had just come out of surgery. She had a cystoscopy. It's when the doctor looks around in her bladder for cancer. She had breast cancer and cancer in her spine and now it seemed it was in her bladder. She was in her mid-fifties. They rolled her into the room. She had tubes attached and drains. Lot of stuff. I was getting the report and introduced myself. Somehow, we bonded. Instantly. She was a really sick lady. She told me a lot about her personal life. She was the mother of nine and had had a lot of sorrow. She had been in an abusive marriage and was divorced. She lost two children. Her ex-husband didn't talk to the children. But she had such a positive outlook, and maybe that's why we bonded, because I'm that way. She was on my floor for four weeks. We had to clean her bladder and we had to hang these big saline bags. Whenever I was on duty, she was my patient. Everyone knew that whatever rooms I was assigned that shift, she was mine. If she wasn't one of my rooms, I'd swap so she was my room. She was my girl. After a while, she was transferred to the oncology unit for chemotherapy. When I was done with my shift, I would go up and see how she was doing. I got to know her kids when they visited. Then there was a two-week period when I wasn't able to go see her. I was so busy and I was also off a week. After I returned, I went up and knocked on the door and her brother answered. She was out of it, totally unresponsive. I started to tear up. Her brother said to me, 'You're going to have to develop thicker skin.' And I said, 'No, I don't. Feeling this way makes me human and it's part of caring as a nurse.' I left crying hysterically and called my mom, who calmed me down. I continued to go up after my shift to visit her. She lay there, unresponsive. Then one day I went up and one of her daughters was there. She said, 'Mom, look who's here.' I thought she was just idly talking to her, the way relatives do even when someone no longer can hear them and respond. But just like that her eyes opened and she said, 'Hadassah!' We both started crying. We started talking and talking and she said she had this infection and she wanted coffee more than anything and they wouldn't give it to her. There are these swabs that we use for cleaning mouths with water. I got a swab and I cleaned her mouth with coffee. I could see the pleasure this gave her, her mouth being cleaned with coffee. I stayed up there for like two hours. Maybe two weeks afterward, I heard the rapid response call for her unit. I had the feeling that it was her. My co-workers looked at me and said: Go. They were coding her. We all knew this was going to happen, but still I can't say how horrible it was for me. She passed. On the thirty-day anniversary of her death, as is Jewish custom, the family had a little meal to mark the anniversary. I was the only non-family member invited. A year-and-a-half later, I got invited to one of her son's wedding. This is nursing."

Wherever there are nurses, stories pour forth. Kristen McConnell, an accomplished neuro intensive care nurse at NYU Langone Medical Center, is one of the smartest people I know. Talking to me one day about nursing, she said something that I found to be especially insightful about this work: "Before I became a nurse, I thought I was too smart to be a nurse. Now I definitely don't think I'm too smart to be a nurse. You have to think a lot. You have to deal with people in the most difficult situations."

She circled around to an encounter that evoked the wonder of nursing. A patient of hers had had a Pipeline stent put in after suffering an aneurysm. Since he was at risk of a stroke, he was on a heparin drip to prevent blood clots, which was to continue into the next day. Someone made an error and the order had expired, so the prior nurse had stopped the drip, not realizing the patient still needed the heparin. McConnell discovered the mistake and got the drip reordered. The patient "didn't freak out," but understood what was going on. Over a year later, he was back on McConnell's unit to have another stent put in. Though he wasn't McConnell's patient, she went to his room to answer a call button. He said, "Hi, Kristen." She expressed surprise that he remembered her. "Of course I remember you," he said, "you saved my life."

Cathy Fogarty, forty-one years a nurse, summoned from her repository a few distinctive stories: "One of my most memorable experiences was the awful case of a twelve-year-old who hung himself. His five-year-old brother found him. This was when I was working at a small community hospital. I can still see his face. I'll always see his face. I can still hear his mother and father. About a year or so later, another nurse had to go to a funeral. I covered for her. I reported to the floor she was working and walked into one of her rooms. There was the mother. She had just given birth to another baby. We looked at each other. She remembered me. And we knew. I said, 'It's no coincidence that I'm here today.' And she said, 'No, it's not.' And we hugged each other."

Then she recounted this macabre one: "Once, a long time ago at a city hospital, someone came in and he was on fire. Actually smoldering, actually smoking. We were throwing water on him to put him out. He had also been shot. You couldn't see that. We only noticed it on an X-ray. Someone had shot him, lit him up, and tossed him into an elevator. When the elevator door opened, someone pulled him out and called the cops. We undressed him and it looked like he had rolls of paper in his pockets. They were two sticks of dynamite. We called the bomb squad. We actually had to close the ER. A nurse put the dynamite on a stretcher and rolled it out to the ambulance bay. He could easily have blown up the ER. He died, so we never did find out what all that was about. But it's safe to assume he was some sort of criminal."

7

Rockland County lies about thirty miles north of Manhattan, bordering the Hudson River. Its name refers to its rocky land. Hadassah Lampert grew up there. Because her mother's doctor practiced out of Lenox Hill, Lampert was born in the very hospital where she now works. Whenever that fact comes up, her supervisors like to point out that they recruit early at Lenox Hill.

Lampert's father is a dentist. Her mother used to teach the deaf at a school in Queens, but now manages the business side of her husband's practice. All four of Lampert's grandparents were Holocaust survivors.

Both her parents are generous, compassionate people. When she was young, Lampert acted as her mother's assistant. She was constantly beside her in the kitchen, acquiring skills. Her mother told her how her own mother wouldn't allow her in the kitchen and she was not going to impose the same restriction on her daughter. When Lampert was eleven, her grandmother died suddenly. It was a holiday and company was coming for dinner. Her mother was in no shape to cook. Lampert prepared the dinner for ten people: salad, sea bass, pasta.

Lampert's sister is nine years younger. Growing up, Lampert spent much of her free time raising her, a fitting preparation for nursing. "She was like my little doll growing up," she said. "I was like her mother. She wasn't always good with that."

Even as a young girl, Lampert knew she wanted to go into health care. It fit her nature and her heartfelt desire to help others. "I like people to be happy," she said. "It's just my general personality." Her impulse was to pursue dentistry because of her father, but she wasn't settled on it. When she was in high school, a day would come when she was at an appointment with her eye doctor. The doctor asked Lampert about her professional ambitions. When Lampert brought up dentistry, her doctor shook her head and said, "Oh, no, I think you should become a nurse."

This stopped Lampert. She hadn't had any meaningful exposure to nurses, and wasn't quite sure exactly what a nurse did. She hadn't played nurse as a child, giving pills to dolls. She'd never read the Helen Wells book series about a wholesome and itinerant nurse named Cherry Ames (*Dude Ranch Nurse, Department Store Nurse, Ski Patrol Nurse*) who solves mysteries. "I didn't really have a good concept of what a nurse was," she said. "I knew they existed. I didn't know what they could do and what they couldn't do."

So she found out everything she could about them. It was eye-opening. It was like the profession was expecting her. Every aspect of nursing appealed to her, and she dismissed the idea of drilling teeth. "I decided this was made for me," she said. "The selflessness of it. The amount that you can grow in it. There are so many areas. There's legal nursing. If you are a tech person, nursing informatics is a degree. At the time, I thought I would do pediatric oncology. But I love the adults. They're so fascinating. I love people."

She enrolled in the nursing program at Touro College in Brooklyn. It was then a two-year program that awarded an associate's degree in nursing. That was sufficient to become an RN, but she desired a bachelor of science in nursing, so she completed that over two additional years through an on-line program at Regis University's nursing school in Denver. The cost of nursing school can be steep and varies widely, depending on whether you go to a public or private school. A two-year associate's degrees can cost between $6,000 to over $100,000; and four-year bachelor's degrees from $40,000 to over $200,000.

Lampert found nursing school demanding. She studied and studied. The reading load was daunting. "They say nursing is one of the hardest degrees," she said. "You have to know so much. You have to know the medical background for everything you're treating." Besides liberal arts courses, she ingested information from courses in anatomy, nutrition, microbiology, pharmacology, and psychology, among other subjects—the technical density of nursing. She learned about the body and about health and about all the things that can go wrong. She learned the proper way to wash your hands. She learned things she didn't know existed to be learned. A buffalo hump is extra fat around the neck.

Augmenting the courses were the anxieties of clinical rotations in a hospital, watching actual nurses do things, and getting the chance to do some things yourself. You developed an iron stomach or tried something else. Besides seeing real humans in pain, there was the simulation lab, where students practiced on silicone robotic mannequins. For decades, nurses had experimented on mannequins, but they didn't move or talk or otherwise actually behave like a sick human being. The robotic ones have pulses, they bleed, they urinate. They squirm and cry and make discontented facial expressions. There are baby robots. Female robots that deliver babies. The instructors will speak through these artificial people. They'll have them identify their problem ("My lungs feel like they're on fire"; "my stomach really hurts"; "I think I'm dying"). They will speak recognizable responses of fear ("I want my mother"; "I want to get out of here"; "I need a priest"). They'll fire repeated questions at the nursing students as they try to follow the protocol they've learned ("What in the world are you doing?" "Why are you doing that?" "Is this going to hurt?"), simulating the distractions and confusion that often accompanies fixing people under pressure. They'll become belligerent ("Why are you so stupid?" "Will you find me a real nurse?"). The professors will also have their fun. They'll have the robot patient say, "Am I alive?"

In her nascent stages of becoming a nurse, Lampert learned to insert catheters in these robots, to give injections, listen to lungs, mend wounds. She discovered how to respond to gruffness and to express compassion for strangers and to see things others didn't see. It was new and thrilling.

It was also weird, since there was no forgetting that these weren't actual people. In the grip of nerves, you might hack off a robot's arm inserting an IV, for instance, which was frowned upon ("Seems we have a problem here, nurse") but not the biggest deal. The robot would simply get a replacement arm before the next nurse stepped in. Still, for nurses in training, confronting one of these synthetic humans could be unsettling. You couldn't kill a pretend person, but you wanted to get it right.

Lampert also found herself asked to conceive projects. She created a self-care basket that was intended to help nurses zone out on their breaks. A manager offered the use of her office and she set up a self-care basket. It contained lavender (its smell has a relaxing effect), reading material, eye masks, a heating pad. Nurses were invited to stop by and make use of anything in the basket. After a period of time, Lampert had them fill out a survey. The results were positive, though as far as Lampert knows, the basket program didn't continue.

Once she had obtained her degree, Lampert needed to pass the National Council Licensure Examination, known as the NCLEX. It's the most important test of a nurse's life. It's a computerized test of primarily multiple-choice questions given at a testing center. It's less a test of basic nursing knowledge than of your ability to analyze situations and apply your knowledge from nursing school. It aims to determine if you can think like a nurse.

Sample questions exist on the internet:

The nurse in the same-day surgery department cares for a 77-year-old woman after a sigmoidoscopy. Which of the following symptoms, if exhibited by the woman an hour after the surgery, would most concern the nurse?

- *The client complains of fullness and pressure in her abdomen.*
- *The client complains of grogginess and thirst.*
- *The client complains of light-headedness and dizziness.*

- *The client complains of mild pain and cramping in her abdomen.*

A nurse is caring for a client in the mental health clinic. A woman comes to the clinic complaining of insomnia and anorexia. The patient tearfully tells the nurse that she was laid off from a job that she had held for 15 years. Which of the following responses, if made by the nurse, is most appropriate?
- *"Did your company give you a severance package?"*
- *"Focus on the fact that you have a healthy, happy family."*
- *"Losing a job is common nowadays."*
- *"Tell me what happened."*

A 67-year-old patient with emphysema becomes restless and confused. Which of the following actions, if taken by the nurse, is BEST?
- *Encourage the patient to perform pursed lip breathing.*
- *Check the patient's temperature.*
- *Assess the patient's potassium level.*
- *Increase the patient's oxygen flow rate to 5 L/min.*

The way it works, you must answer at least seventy-five questions within six hours. You could potentially get asked as many as two hundred and sixty-five questions, the quantity depending on how well you are doing. As you get answers right, the questions increase in difficulty for that section; they get easier after a wrong answer. It's possible to pass after answering the bare minimum and also to fail after being asked just seventy-five questions. Once the computer has made its assessment, the screen goes black. But you don't find out the verdict for forty-eight hours.

Lampert is not one to study for tests well in advance. "I'm always a last-minute person," she said. "I'm best under pressure."

She bought a package of five thousand sample questions and studied for a week. It was not normal to study for only a week.

It was normal to get a good night's sleep the day before the exam and consume a robust breakfast. Lampert did not sleep well. She had no breakfast. While her mother drove her into Manhattan to the testing place, she munched on a Snickers bar. She was literally shaking as she arrived.

As the questions popped up, she answered quickly, not usually with tremendous certainty. After seventy-five questions, the magic minimum possible for the computer's algorithm to judge her competence, the computer went black. An hour had lapsed. She was sure that she had failed.

Dejected, she drifted outside to find her mother. So little time had passed that she hadn't yet found a parking place.

Two days later, her results arrived. She had passed. She

stared at the paper in disbelief. Then she began shrieking and jumping up and down. Her thrilled mother said, "My daughter is a nurse."

She applied to Lenox Hill and was hired in February 2011. Her first assignment was the night shift in the neurology unit. Orientation protocols for new nurses vary by state and hospital. For her first three months, she worked under the tutelage of a preceptor, an experienced nurse. Heart hammering, Lampert performed under her preceptor's watchful eyes, digesting her explanations and advice, and gradually taking on more tasks and patients until she gained her footing. Then, her skills proven, her preceptor became her co-worker. "It was the scariest thing," she said. "Suddenly you're doing everything. You're the one. But it was so exciting."

She loved the medicine floors and their various manifestations. The pace was slower than the ER; you saw patients for days or weeks, not hours. "It was an amazing foundation," she said. "You can hone your skills. You can really learn medications. You learn how to connect with patients. You do it by just making conversation on something small, something you have in common. You don't just go, 'I'm going to put in an IV' or 'I'm going to give you an injection.' You talk about anything but that. You talk about life. On the units, you see the same patients every day. They are often there for a while. I still remember this Italian guy who was very stubborn. He wouldn't listen to anyone. He wouldn't listen to his wife. He listened to me. Tough love, I guess. And I connect with people easily. He hated getting out of bed. Hated walking around. I told him, 'You're not going to get better if you don't get up.' He got up. He had prostate cancer that spread to his kidneys. He was maybe fifty. He went up to oncology and I visited him there sometimes. I would play *Words With Friends* with his wife. This is years later, and we still play occasionally."

Nursing gladdened her. As she found herself perfecting her skills in her own small piece of the medical world, she resolved that this was her life's career. Eventually, she came to the ER. It was a significant change. By and large, floor nurses and ER nurses are of two minds. Floor nurses think ER nurses don't do anything. ER nurses think floor nurses don't do anything. It's a long-standing, ingrained culture clash, persisting from the fact that, as Cathy Fogarty put it, "no one walks in the other's shoes."

In the ER, Lampert was required to do a yearlong fellowship. For three months, she was in a classroom and doing simulations, even planning for a hypothetical bombing or bus crash that would overrun the ER with mass casualties. Then came six months under the watch of a preceptor, gaining independence, followed by three months on her own with no more than five patients. It was a different experience. On the floors, patients arrived with a diagnosis; you knew what was wrong with them. In the ER, you saw mysteries. Everything was at top speed. A to-do list without end. She hadn't imagined it would suit her, but she fell under its grip. "It's always different, challenging," she said. "Even though you see a lot of the same things, it's always in a different way. It's nurse-driven. I like the teamwork. I like the pace. A lot of critical thinking, you always have to be on your toes. I actually thought I would hate it, because everyone makes out the ER to be a beast with heartless nurses who send patients up with dirty, bloody sheets. They think ER nurses are going through the motions. There's that misconception among a lot of nurses. That you've gone to the dark side. If they see patients come up half-dressed and the IV bag is not perfectly labeled, they think you're careless. They don't realize you're scrambling to save people's lives. That's what we're doing every day, saving lives."

8

It could get chilly in the ER—useful for defeating bacteria—so it was good to have a sweatshirt. Patients burrowed beneath blankets to beat the shivers.

The man was elfin, with wispy hair and heavy eyelids. He was sixty-five, but looked older. The ER seemed to have passed the day's crescendo of activity. Beds, though, remained stuffed in the halls and shoved against the nurses' station, which is where this man found himself. He had pain of undetermined origin that began in his back and radiated out to his thigh. The doctor said to give him some morphine, which Lampert did, while he awaited testing. It calmed him down.

Yet when Lampert looked in on him fifteen minutes later, she found him crying. His shoulders were shaking. His legs were flapping up and down. Something had dented his hopes.

She searched his uptilted face, patches of moisture glistening on his cheeks. "What's the matter?" she asked him.

"I'm scared," he said. He tried to say more but his face

tightened and the words got jammed up and he burst back into a geyser of tears.

All around, the rumble of the room continued unabated, but Lampert's attention was arrested by the needs of this man. She lowered the side railing on his bed, perched on the mattress edge, and gripped his hand, his knuckly fingers.

"You're scared?" she said. "Why are you scared? Don't be scared."

"I'm so scared. I don't know why. I'm scared."

He kept sobbing. He pulled on his lip.

"Everyone gets a little scared of the emergency room," Lampert said softly. "It's normal."

She rubbed the side of his face. "There're a lot of people here and I think you got overwhelmed. Don't be scared. We're here and we're going to take good care of you. How about we take your vital signs and be sure everything's okay?"

"Okay. You'll take care of me for sure?"

In her gentlest voice, she said, "Yes, of course I'll take care of you."

He quieted down, appreciative of the concern. Sometimes the kind words a nurse says, and how she says them, the potency of small moments, can surpass the contribution of any medicine. Hand-holding is nursing. Touching a patient's face is nursing. There aren't pills for everything. After she checked his vitals, Lampert said, "All your signs look good.

You're okay. I'm here for you. I'll come check on you in a little bit."

She patted his shoulder and slid silently away. He closed his eyes and turned over into sleep.

When observers of nurses talk about what separates a great nurse from an ordinary nurse, they inevitably get around to caring. Nurses who last at their work all possess proficient technical skills. Not all have empathy. Budding nurses are taught about the difference between empathy and sympathy, how they need to relate to patients without becoming sorry for them and overly invested in them. When they empathize, they exude compassion. Nurses hear about Jean Watson, a nursing theorist, who put forth her Theory of Human Caring, that the foundation of nursing is establishing a caring relationship with patients, "that humans cannot be treated as objects." She posited as well that nurses must care for themselves in order to care for others. It can be an undefined line, how much you find yourself entwined with someone.

When I spoke to Lampert about how she connected to patients, she said, "It's seeing the patient as a whole, not just the cough in bed three."

Asked what made a bad nurse, she said, "The lack of passion is a big part of it. People who view it as a job are bad nurses. They do all the things they're supposed to do. They give the medications. They hang the IVs. They check all the boxes. But that's it. That's all they do. Bad nurses have skills. They don't have the empathy."

When I asked Irene Macyk, the hospital's chief nursing officer, why Lampert excelled, she told me, "You feel her caring. When she's around, you feel her humanism. She looks at you. She wants to help you. Most nurses are as clinically skilled as Hadassah. What makes her stand out is that sense of caring. It's palpable."

Cathy Fogarty told me: "It's her passion. She loves what she does. She went into nursing for the right reason. She wanted to do something to help others. And that shows in everything she does. I wish I could clone her. I can teach a monkey to do some of the things that we do. I can't teach compassion and empathy."

Show you care. Show it to everyone, equal doses all around. As Dr. Duroseau explained to me: "Patient number fifty should get the same level of compassion as patient number one. No matter how tired you are. It's got to be the same as when you come in and are full of energy and want to save the world."

A talkative seventeen-year-old arrived with her attentive parents, complaining of persistent stomach pains. Nervously and volubly, she told Lampert her story: "Last night when I was lying on my stomach, my stomach was hurting. I thought, okay, it's hurting because I'm lying on my stomach.

So I turned over and fell asleep and then I woke up and it was hurting again. I tried to fall back asleep but no, it was hurting. Then I was a little nauseous. I didn't want to go to the emergency room, but my parents insisted. The emergency room sounds really scary."

Lampert said, "Well, you're here. Emergency rooms do sound scary, but they're not. You're going to get through this and we'll find out what's wrong. This will involve some needles."

Lampert told her she would be inserting an IV to take blood for lab tests, then she would receive a CAT scan. The notion of a needle entering her arm froze her. Lampert talked her down, gave her standard refrain of how she, too, a nurse living in a world of needles was "a baby when it comes to getting needles." (Lampert told me that she did indeed fear needles for many years, but has become more tolerant. The confession, though, often takes the squeamishness from patients. "It's all about the drama," she said.)

The girl's whole body jittered and she began to cry. "No, no, no," she said.

Lampert said, "Now look at me. Once I have this in, I can take blood. I can give you intravenous fluids. I can give you medicine."

Her father said, "It's for your own good."

The girl glared at him and said, "Daddy, can you please

step out. You already made me cry once since we've been here. I don't need you here to make me cry again."

A leaden air dropped over them. Sheepishly, the admonished father stepped out. The girl wiped her damp eyes with her hand. She blinked excessively. Her mother suggested she put on her headphones and listen to music.

"Yes, good idea," Lampert said. "Can I listen, too?"

As Lampert prepared the needle, she asked the girl if she had considered what she wanted to be.

"Not really," she said.

"Maybe today you're going to decide you want to be a nurse. You never know. I'm going to put the IV in now. You'll feel a little pinch."

"I may or may not scream," the girl said.

"You can scream," Lampert said. "The only thing I ask you is not to move."

"I'm going to turn the music up so loud I'm probably not going to hear you."

The needle pierced the skin and disappeared. The girl screamed. "It hurts. It hurts."

"It's over," Lampert said. "It's in. That's it. You're brave. You're so brave. Take a deep breath."

Her mood significantly downshifted. "Look, how long am I going to be here?"

"A couple of hours probably. But hey, you get to hang out with me. It doesn't get better than that."

The girl just looked at Lampert.

Once Lampert left to update the girl's chart, the girl was telling her mother, "I hate you. I actually hate you. Go away."

The tests ultimately were negative. The girl simply had a stomachache and a parent problem.

Lampert's mind slid away from the stomachache girl when, shortly afterward, a plastic surgeon requested her in one of the procedure rooms to hold a head.

A five-year-old had a deep cut in his chin that required stitches. He was not a logical candidate to take it calmly. His parents were there to hold his arms down. The surgeon needed Lampert to keep his head still and to soothe him, talk about this or that or anything but the fact that a needle was going in and out of his chin.

"Hi, what's going on?" Lampert said to him, squeezing his shoulder and shifting into High-Calm Mode. "You fell? Were you playing?"

"Sort of," the boy said. He had a cute, round face.

"Doing boy things, huh?" she said, smiling at him knowingly. "I have a nephew your age. He does boy things, too."

At home, he had been watching TV. His father entered the room. Gladdened by his arrival, he decided to leap off the couch into his dad's arms. He neglected, however, to signal his intention. He dove headfirst onto the floor.

"Were you watching *PAW Patrol*?" Lampert asked, referencing the cartoon about a team of heroic dogs ("No job is too big, no pup is too small").

"Yeah."

"*PAW Patrol*, on the double," Lampert said.

The doctor glanced at her. "How do you know that?"

"I have a nephew."

His father held down his elbows and Lampert clamped her hands on each side of his head. Neither parent could look as the doctor injected the boy with an anesthetic and began to stitch up the wound. The boy responded with a deafening scream.

Intently, Lampert tilted her head over his face. She spoke to him with noticeable affection. She said, "It's going to be okay. It really will be. You're so brave."

"I'm in pain. I'm in pain."

The doctor said, "The worst part is over."

"You're so good," Lampert said, impulsively keeping the air filled with words. "You're going to get a treat. What would you like for a treat?"

He continued to cry and try to squirm away from the doctor's needle.

His mother said, "Do you want me to sing to you? You want me to sing what I was singing in the car? Remember I was singing, 'You Are My Sunshine'?"

"Make him stop. Make him stop."

Lampert said, "I don't think I've ever seen anyone as brave as you."

His mother said, "You are so brave. You're the bravest boy there ever was."

"I want to go."

His mother said, "You want me to count to five hundred? Remember Daddy counted to five hundred and eighty-one in the car last week. Want me to do it? One, two, three . . ."

"It's scary."

Lampert said, "It is scary. But it doesn't hurt. And you are so brave."

The nervous mother said, "They're going to need an ambulance to take me home afterward."

The boy's crying continued uninhibited. "I can't stand it," he screamed. "I can't stand it."

"It's almost over," Lampert said. "No one could like this. You're so brave."

"I can't breathe."

"Almost done," Lampert said. "I see you have a *PAW Patrol* watch too. Wow, is that cool."

The father was investigating the condition of the wall and the ceiling, looking anywhere but at the doctor putting stitches in his little boy's chin.

"It's super scary," the boy cried.

Lampert kept offering assuagements: "I know, but you don't have to be scared. I'm here. We're all here."

The mother said, "I'll count to one hundred twenty and we'll be done."

The doctor said, "Better make it two hundred."

"I'll count slow. One, two, three . . ."

The boy said, "I feel sad."

"I know you're sad," Lampert said.

"I had a sad day."

"You had a sad day," the mother said. "Tomorrow will be a happy day."

At last, the procedure was completed. Lampert told him, "You were so brave and so wonderful. Everyone should be as brave as you."

"Bye, bye," he told Lampert.

While Lampert finds patients freely open up to her, she generally reveals little about herself to them. "I never get too personal," she told me. "They need me. I don't need them. I'll connect about my hobbies. Movies. It's not professional to get too personal about yourself. But patients do get very personal. They want to know your relationship status. I'll go to introduce myself and while I'm putting in the IV, they'll say, 'Are you single?' It gets asked all the time. All the time. It's the most common question. They come into the ER and they lose all inhibition. They're like babies. I understand. I mean, you lose all respect here. The minute you come in you get undressed and go around with a gown that opens in the back."

Nurses evolve. They set boundaries to shield themselves from the emotional impact so patients don't burden them. You can't do this line of work if you enter every patient's life and never leave them. "It's very easy at the beginning of your career to take everything personally," Lampert said. "I guess I did that, too. You learn. It's okay to cry with a patient and to feel with them. But you don't want the patient to be comforting you."

The ER in full swing, an IV challenge presented itself. A man who was in bed 17 was known as a "hard stick," someone who was dehydrated or had been stuck with needles so often that the veins had collapsed and wouldn't hold an IV. IVs, ubiquitous in hospitals, are vital for administering fluids and medications. By Lampert's description, "Nurses do them a million times a day." Some, though, prove trickier than others. One of her fellow nurses asked Lampert if she wanted to try with the ultrasound machine that does a sound-wave test.

She said that eight people had already attempted and failed to place an IV in the man's ruined veins. The numbers did not auger well for a ninth try. The man was a chemotherapy patient and thus had been stuck myriad times. Ever confident, Lampert was unfazed by the serial failures.

"Sure," she said.

She said to me, "People hear ultrasound machine and they think babies. But it has other purposes." Her plan was to run it across the man's arm to hunt for a deep-enough vein.

Intent on her task, Lampert assembled what she needed from the supply cabinet and piled it into a pink plastic container. Following sterile procedures, she yanked on beige vinyl one-use-only gloves. Wheeling the ultrasound machine next to the man in his curtained domain, she locked eyes with him and said, "How are you? My name is Hadassah. I'm a nurse."

"Hi there," the man said. "I'm a patient."

He was lanky with a stubbled face and leathery skin. He wore a railroad engineer's cap.

"I'm going to use this machine to try to find a deep vein," Lampert told him. "It's going to be fine." She gave him a wide smile. The soft skills of medicine can matter as much as the technical ones. Your posture. Your tone. How you discuss a patient's concerns. How you tell them good news and bad news, especially the bad news.

Wondering about her medical authority, the man asked, "Are you the head?"

She laughed. "No, I'm not the head, not even close," she said. "But I know how to use this."

A relative was visiting, but excused herself. Watching a needle go into skin wasn't for her. The ER had no limit on visitors, and Lampert liked their presence as an extra source of information. When the ER got excessively busy, though, unofficial protocol was to keep it to two visitors per patient.

Lampert got right to it. She ran the probe at a consistent pace over the man's right arm, his thready muscles, while keeping her eyes fixed on the machine's monitor. After several minutes, Lampert pointed out a vein.

"That looks like a winner," the other nurse said.

Lampert readied a needle and stuck it in the discovered vein. The man closed his eyes and turned away.

It wouldn't hold. A lot of his veins had been used many times. Lampert said to him, "Pin cushion, huh?"

The man just grunted.

In the bed beside him, barely a few feet away, a spindly woman was exclaiming in a stony voice, "Ooh, ooh, ooh. I'm having a really ridiculous day. This is the most ridiculous day of my life. Ooh, ooh, ooh."

Amid the commotion of the ER, another nurse was announcing that her patient had been flipped. If someone "flips," it means they've been admitted. Nurses will say things like, "Bed 3 was flipped," or, "I'm going to flip this lady." Flipping goes on all day. A doctor whirled past, lamenting in an irritated aside about poor progress with a patient.

"There's a lot of tension down here," Lampert said to me.

Lampert cranked the bed lower. Dutifully, she ran the probe over the man's arm again, identified a new vein. This time the invading needle held.

"There," she said. "How do you feel?"

He offered a look of gratitude. "Good. A win."

"A win for me, too," Lampert said.

The other nurse said, "Strong work, Hadassah, as always."

Encountering the doctor treating the man, Lampert said, "We're good."

"You got it?"

"Yes."

"You're the best."

9

Wouldn't you know, she got a stroke code when her shift was nearly done. It was a high-attendance day. After finishing with her patient tasks, Lampert scrunched herself in front of an available computer terminal, fellow nurses only inches away, and began punching in information. Her fingers jabbed at keys, filling crowds of boxes, her head bobbing.

"We do this all day," Lampert said. "All day, every day."

Charting. The meticulous detail of a patient's condition and all that had been done to heal him. Homework on the run. Every medication had to be charted. Vital signs. The location of a patient's IV. Their level of pain. Did they leave with someone? What patient education were they given? Did they arrive with a PICC line? Was it deaccessed and reaccessed? Are they a risk for fall? This went on for patient after patient. The narrative of their medical lives.

It was the obligatory drudgery of nursing. All nurses must do charting for their patients on electronic flow sheets, the frequency and detail varying by the severity of the condition. Over the years, it's gotten more extensive, more things asked, much of it demanded by insurers and hospitals for billing purposes. Patients have gotten sicker, meaning more to include. A good deal of it is checking boxes; otherwise notes must be written. It swallows up time, nurses spending more of their day charting than doing anything else, often the majority of their shift. It's a significant factor in nurse burnout, and all nurses complain endlessly about it. I was reminded of a mantra I had heard: "I came. I cared. I charted."

When charting was done on paper, nurses completed it beside the patient. Now that it's electronic, nurses in the ER spend the bulk of their time before a computer terminal. Some hospitals have added handheld computers so nurses can stay with the patient while charting, something Lenox Hill was hoping to do in the next year.

Lampert kept punching in information. Much of it was expressed in medical terminology and acronyms, unintelligible to the laity. Boxes and spaces to fill for everything. The use of restraints. One-to-ones. Doctor notes. Security concerns. Suicide risk. Education assessment. Past surgical history. Personal history. Social history. Substance abuse history. Triage notes. Nurse's notes. Triage pain assessment numbers. The AVPU scale telling how alert and responsive the person is. One day a nurse lamented to me how there were four places where she had to document that her patient was unconscious. And yet nurses hear nurse managers scolding them at shift change meetings that they're not documenting this or that.

When I asked Cathy Fogarty what nurses least like to do, she answered immediately, "Charting would be number one."

Vitals must be continually updated. A certain amount of judgment is involved, but a really sick patient in the ER has vitals checked every five to ten minutes, then every fifteen minutes, then every hour, the frequency reduced as they become stabilized. Level 2 patients tend to get vitals checked at least every two hours, Level 3 at least every four hours ("but we do it far more often," Lampert said). Levels 4 and 5 are checked when they come in and within an hour of discharge. It's hard with multiple patients under your purview. "I've had as many as seven or eight patients at a time, other times I've had four," Lampert said. In the ER, staffing guidelines are to try to assign no more than six patients to each nurse, two if the patients are critical. Nurse-to-patient guidelines matter. Some studies have concluded that too-high ratios raise the odds of patients dying.

"There's a lot of charting, there's no denying that," Lampert said. "A lot. Charting is frustrating and annoying, but it has to be done. There's a motto we all learn that if you haven't documented it, it wasn't done. If a nurse is called to court as a witness, it's crucial to have good documentation of what was done because it could be years later and would be hard to remember if it was not documented. I was never called to court and don't know anyone who has been, though I know it does happen."

Nursing shifts are long enough at twelve hours, yet there is so much charting that it is not uncommon for Lampert and the other nurses to stay chained to their monitors beyond the end of their workday, done scuttling from room to room and sapped of energy, to complete their updates.

Now she had to pause her charting to give some medication to two of her patients—albuterol here, antibiotics there—after which she would have to chart that.

Patient safety is something nurses hear about repeatedly. In nursing school, they are taught to question whether everything they do is safe. Lampert told me: "Safe means following evidence-based practices. Always question a medication. Just because a doctor orders it doesn't mean it's right. They order it for one patient and it's meant for another patient. They order the wrong dose. It doesn't happen every day, but it happens."

As a precaution against mistakes, Lampert and other hospital personnel identify patients by scanning the bar codes on their wristbands. Before they do anything to a patient, they ask the patient's name and date of birth, checking it against their wristband (sometimes they will even have them spell their first and last names).

In nursing school, to avoid harming patients, nurses have imprinted into their brains to follow the classic "Five Rights" of medication administration, to do them without thinking: the right patient, the right drug, the right dose, the right route, and the right time. Often, nurses are conditioned to abide by additional rights: the right documentation, the right reason, the right response, the right to refuse, the right education.

Mistakes still happen. It is easier than new nurses can imagine to do harm with the wrong medication or by not being sufficiently alert to warning signs in someone's condition. Are they becoming hypotensive? Is that catheter in too long, risking infection? What about that breathing tube? It's why you hear nurses say, "That's not safe" or "Let's do this, just to be safe."

"There are so many things to be careful about or patients can be harmed," Lampert said. "You need to check IVs to see that they're working. If the patient is bedbound, and you don't clean them, if you don't turn them, if you don't walk them. You have to keep checking that a patient hasn't ripped any tubes out."

A doctor collared Lampert. He questioned her about whether a patient in bed 3 got what he needed. Doctors and nurses have had a fluctuating, hierarchical relationship over the years. Still do. "Some really respect nurses and some don't," Lampert told me. "For the most part, I've had very good collaborations. And just as the doctor needs to trust the nurse, the nurse needs to trust the doctor. Usually there's mutual respect. Sometimes there's the doctor who goes, 'I'm the doctor. What are you doing? I'm the doctor.' Some doctors are more abrasive. They feel entitled. They have to have the last say. You can't argue back to them, even if they're wrong. Other doctors ask my opinion about patients and what to do. And I feel free to question a doctor. And they will change their mind or explain why they're doing something. I think most doctors know they would be nowhere without nurses."

Fogarty told me this about the relationship: "It's the best I've seen it. They see each other as team members. It used to be more of a hierarchy. Doctors saw themselves as above nurses. When I started, if I was sitting at the nurses' station and a doctor walked in, I had to stand and give him my chair."

"Why has it changed?"

"An understanding that no one does this alone."

The reason a doctor can visit a patient sporadically is because they can trust the nurses to be doing it constantly, taking stock and summoning them if they're needed.

"The nurse is the first contact with the patient," Lampert told me. "You always have to be on the lookout for abnormalities. A big part of nursing is nurse intuition. It serves as a signal that something is wrong. It's why you need to trust nurses."

Any number of times while I was following her, Lampert demonstrated the importance of a nurse's intuition, that it takes more than measuring oxygen levels and temperature to determine the condition of a patient. She pointed me to a recent study of nurses by Mayo Clinic researchers. It found that a nurse's sense about whether a patient's condition was likely to worsen in the next twenty-four hours—what researchers measured using a "worry factor" score—was remarkably reliable in predicting decline and important in saving lives. "I think every nurse has a level of it," Lampert said. "A good nurse is pretty much always on point."

As Dr. Duroseau summarized it when I asked him about how doctors saw nurses: "We all know as physicians that nurses save us. They're the eyes and ears of the hospital. They spend more time with the patients."

One afternoon, I took a break from following Lampert's routines and went to see Irene Macyk, the chief nursing officer, who oversees the fifteen hundred nurses at three of Northwell's locations. Her office was in the administration wing, near the back entrance beside the security office. She's an ebullient woman with a personality that enwraps you.

She told me how she entered nursing. In school, she favored math and physics. Her dream was to become an astronaut. Summers, she spent time with her grandmother in Brooklyn, and one summer when Macyk was in college, her cousin was there. She was a pediatric nurse doing child therapy in a hospital, helping children with chronic illnesses and abused children cope with their disturbing circumstances, bringing sunshine into dark lives. "I thought it was the coolest thing in the world," Macyk told me.

Just like that, she switched her major to nursing. She was determined to become a pediatric nurse, and she did that for a long while before moving into management.

I asked her about the career tracks of nurses, and she said, "The new generation of nurses is always looking for the next thing. They may do clinical work for six years or so, then go back for their master's and become nurse practitioners. Then there is a big segment—the majority of nurses—who want to always be a clinical nurse. They never want to leave the bedside." Nurses so disposed like Macyk move into management as head nurses or chief nurses.

"Who makes a good nurse?" I asked Macyk.

"Someone who's really authentic," she said. "Someone who cares to create relationships."

"What stops someone from becoming a good nurse?"

"The ones who don't take the time to get to know the patient and to create a relationship," she said. "If someone is sick and frustrated, how do I get them to really say what's going on? You have to see more than someone's blood pressure is up and they're not urinating."

Macyk said that nurses do so much more than people imagine. "People think they give me the meds and they help me get a gown on and go to the bathroom," she said. "When they're dressing you and helping you to the bathroom, they're looking at your gait. They're looking at whether your eyes are yellow. Your skin color. When you breathe, do you flare your nostrils? They're looking at your neck. Do you strain when you breathe? Are you breathing through your nose? Two hours ago, you weren't pulling on your neck. Now you're pulling on your neck. It could mean you're having trouble getting air into your airway. Nurses are looking for swelling. Bleeding. Discoloration. Are your eyes starting to droop? Is your sclera, the white of your eye, bloodshot? People think nurses do things. They're assessing. The whole assessment is like a surveillance. We're like a surveillance machine. That's the magic of nursing."

She grinned and said, "Right now, as we're talking, I'm assessing you."

I said, "How do I look?"

She said, "Okay so far."

Macyk explained that while nurses learn basic assessment

in nursing school, they refine it on the job. Experienced nurses pick up things that new nurses don't. Their miss rate is much lower. Academics talk about a pathway of clinical proficiency that nurses follow.

Patricia Benner, a nursing theorist, has written about this progression, most notably in her book, *From Novice to Expert: Excellence and Power in Clinical Nursing Practice*. She applies the Dreyfus model of how learners acquire skills to nursing, and describes how nurses pass through five stages: novice, when the new nurse lacks confidence and needs constant physical and verbal cues; advanced beginner, when knowledge accumulates and her performance is marginally acceptable; competent, when the nurse is confident, consistent, and efficient; proficient, when situations are viewed as wholes rather than groupings of pieces, which sharpens decision-making; and finally, expert, when a nurse draws on her deep understanding of a situation to make accurate decisions without wasting time on ill-advised alternatives.

In fits and starts, staring down the capriciousness of sickness, nurses move through the stages. Generally speaking, a new nurse needs up to five years to reach the level of expert.

10

There was that shrill voice again. And again. Its harshness rattled your teeth. The short, dour woman in bed 1 had arrived after a fall, a possible broken hip. She was waiting for a CAT scan. She wondered when it would happen. She wondered even more if she would ever eat again.

She screamed to the world at large: "I'm hungry. I'm hungry. Give me food."

Lampert hurried over to console her. She let her know that she could not eat until they determined if she had a fracture, please calm down.

"Give me food," she screamed.

"You have to stop screaming," Lampert said.

The woman shot her a look of curt distrust: "Give me food."

Some patients arrive at the ER and fancy that, finally, they've acquired the servants they've always deserved. Their egos become fatter than the beds.

"We can't give you food yet," Lampert said. "You need to wait."

The woman compressed her face into a sneer. She had thick, cracked lips, and she said: "Fuck you."

"That's not a nice thing to say to me," Lampert said.

The woman jerked forward in the bed. "Shut up. I hate you."

Lampert allowed that to move past her, letting it go at, "Okay, you hate me."

The hectoring woman simmered down. Lampert returned to the refuge of the nurses' station, feeling the woman's scowling stare on her neck. She had barely sat down to examine some charts when a renewed volley of unfiltered demands reclaimed her attention. The woman was becoming a tape loop: "Give me food. I'm hungry. I'm hungry. Fuck you." Other nurses perked up, taking in the episode.

Lampert told her, "Can you stop screaming and stop cursing?"

"Fuck you," the woman yelled. "You never went to college."

"I never went to college?"

"You don't know nothing. You're stupid. No one is as stupid as you. I hate you."

This harangue went on for a while, reaching a stand-off only when the woman was rolled into the radiology suite. Cleared of a fracture, she was fed a plastic-wrapped sandwich and ginger ale and discharged, her only persisting condition a rude mouth.

Nursing can be a fraught endeavor. Nurses see people at their worst and their most vulnerable. They want to be healed without being hurt further. For often misguided reasons, some patients bring demands that no nurse could fulfill and feel there is no uncrossable line in expressing their displeasure. Some are impolite. Some are defiant. Some bring nurses to tears and even frighten them. Some attack them.

Bullying and incivility are ongoing issues. In a recent American Nurses Association survey, 20 percent of respondents said they had been physically abused by a patient; more than 55 percent said they had been verbally abused. Although few nurses reported being physically abused by relatives of patients, 40 percent said they had been verbally abused. More than a third also said they had been subjected to "horizontal violence," verbally assaulted by another employee or health care worker. It is not uncommon for nurses to bully fellow nurses. All nurses know the showy idiom "nurses eat their young," which captures the troubling nastiness—refusing to help them, belittling them in front of patients—that certain experienced nurses inflict on new nurses.

Talk to nurses at various hospitals and stories aplenty emerge of patients abusing them. Swear words strung together in every imaginable combination. Urine hurled at them. One nurse told me of a pugnacious man who incorrectly became convinced that she was going to order an operation on his heart that he knew would kill him. He removed his belt from his pants and began waving it over his head like a lariat, warning her, "Don't come near me. Don't come near me."

Another nurse told me about an unmoored patient who felt his nurse was not responsive enough when he wanted a drink. He warned her that he was going to retrieve his gun and come back and shoot her. Then he punched the wall hard enough to open a hole in it and said, "What if I punched you like that?"

Still another nurse, in fact, told me about being punched in the stomach, after telling the patient he couldn't leave the hospital. One nurse had been slapped hard on several occasions, once with a copy of *National Geographic*. A woman batted a nurse with her cane. A nurse was hit by a meatloaf sandwich. Another had her temple cut open by a flung cellphone—Samsung. The missile that struck yet another nurse was a generous helping of string beans. Patients have called 911 from their beds, wanting their nurse jailed for slow response. Nurses have been stabbed. They have been held hostage at gunpoint.

Among hospital personnel, nurses bear the brunt of this brutish behavior because, as the front line, they have the most contact with patients. Nearly 90 percent of nurses are women, more likely to be targets of violence.

The turbulent landscape of the emergency room is especially prone to histrionics. Patients and family members insist on the elimination of pain—now; this second. Many patients show up with mental illnesses or head injuries that unleash dangerous behavior.

Cathy Fogarty told me, "It's worse than I've ever seen it. They are cursed at. They are yelled at. They are spit at. We recently started having a New York City cop in the ER for that reason. We've had patients swing at and hit nurses. They throw things at nurses—anything they can get their hands on. I've had rooms destroyed. Monitors ripped off the wall. It's not just the ER. It's all over the hospital."

What sets them off?

"Patients come here with the expectation they will get pain medication," she said. "That's the main thing. Some are mental patients, but most are just people who lose control because we didn't meet their expectations, which are unreasonable."

I asked Fogarty why she thought such attacks had gotten worse?

"Because it's tolerated," she said. "Society accepts it. It's a value change. Teachers take this from students. It's all professions. It starts with kids. In the past, people would get angry and say bad things. Now they take it to a new level. It's not only patients. It's family members too. We had a family member take a swing at a nurse. The daughter of a woman patient who didn't think her mother was getting better fast enough. We have pressed charges against violent patients. I'm telling you, nurses get threatened every day. They hear, 'I'm going to find you and get you.' We had a nurse followed the other day."

One Sunday morning, Lampert and the other nurses were discussing a man who had been roundly cursing the nurses. One nurse said she came to his bedside and told him, "I have your seizure medication," and he said to her, "Well, about fucking time."

She ignored his coarseness and said, "How do you want to take it?"

And he said, "Well, you've got to put them in my mouth, don't you, you moron."

"Oh my god," Lampert said. "And we have to say, 'Yes, that's right, sir.' "

When I spoke to Lampert about nurse abuse, she told me, "We're always apologizing for something—even if we didn't do it. We're apologizing for how they feel. We're apologizing for the wait. We're apologizing for there being no beds. We're apologizing because it's raining out."

New nurses tend to take incivility, even tame rebukes,

personally, but Lampert said you learn to bat these insults away. "Nurses are verbally abused every day," she told me. "A lot of cursing. Nothing gets taken personally. You can't take it personally or you couldn't function. But it's not always easy to not judge them. Some patients are really mean."

How does she deal with them?

"I do it by thinking, everyone is somebody's child. Everyone was a baby once. That gets me through it. The bottom line is the patient is the customer. And they can go anywhere, especially in today's health care."

Only once did Lampert experience physical abuse, struck in the back by a patient in a rage for some now blurry reason. Lampert stepped away and security intervened.

"We live in a very volatile society," Lampert told me. "I just think people feel more entitled. They have different values. They come to us for help, but they act like we're the problem. It's the minority who abuse us, but it doesn't feel like the minority. The ones we're moaning about at the end of a shift are not the nice people but the nasty ones."

"Have you ever lost your cool and yelled at a patient?" I asked.

"My losing my cool is saying, 'We're not going to have this conversation anymore,' and I walk away," she said. "I'm not one to yell. I'm not a yeller. This is part of the job. Nursing is not all glamour. You tell someone you're a nurse and they think it's like *ER* or *Grey's Anatomy*. It's not all nice. It's hard. It's dirty. Physically and emotionally, it's a lot. You have to really care about helping people, being part of something bigger, doing something for society. You can't go into nursing and just exist like in some jobs. You have to have passion for it. Not all nurses do. They're the ones who are always complaining, who are always miserable. Nursing is a practice. It's not a job. You can't view it as a job. You have to view it as a practice. And there's a reason it's called a practice. You're always learning something new."

11

The wizened woman with bristling eyebrows lay unconscious. She was curled up, her head bowed and aslant. A stuporous man with horribly swollen feet was having trouble breathing and occupied the next bed. Two people in rebelling bodies tired of arguing with disease, in the tight sphere between life and death.

Everyone was scrambling, the ER having just received a burst of patients. Lampert was working on the woman's chart when a doctor told her he was calling a Code Fusion. She was bleeding internally and her family wanted a transfusion. Her hemoglobin level had dropped to 3 grams per deciliter. Normal for a woman was 12 to 15.5.

Lampert and a fellow nurse hustled to her bedside. She told the other nurse, "This wasn't supposed to happen. The initial conversation was comfort care and it blew up to this. Oh well. It is what it is."

There are many codes in the hospital, something like fifteen in all. Code Fusion is for a blood transfusion. The famous Code Blue, of course, is cardiac arrest. Code White is pediatric cardiac arrest. Code 100 is neonatal resuscitation. Code Red is fire. Code Amber is pediatric infant abduction. Code Green Active is active shooter. Code Flight is adult patient is missing or has "eloped," meaning the person, without preannouncement, simply took off.

Not everyone who comes to this room leaves. The woman was accompanied by her husband and other family members. She was eighty-eight. She had advanced, untreatable cancer among other grave conditions, her life being pulled irreversibly to whatever lay next. Her family recognized that doctors could no longer patch her up and had agreed to take no more steps to keep her alive. Mortal decision-making, never easy, but made. As it turned out, though, she had a private nurse there, a woman moonlighting from another hospital. When the hemoglobin level dropped, the nurse convinced the family to do a transfusion. Neither the attending doctor nor Lampert felt that course of action was wise, but they needed to obey the family's wishes.

"That's so common in the ER," Lampert told me. "The family reverses itself. When they actually face life and death—and this is literally life and death—they can't make the call."

Duels like this over when to let go of someone and permit them to die, frequently prickly in nature, go on between siblings, friends, ex-wives, ex-husbands, and all combinations of interested parties. One person feels they know best or they hold more love or they simply relish being argumentative. All too often these disputes occur over comatose or incoherent patients unable to speak for themselves. If they could, they would wish away the sometimes-tortuous medical invasions that won't bring back their health. It was a troubling issue of medicine, the questionable lavishing of medical technology on people done with living.

This particular duel, Lampert suspected, was not based on the private nurse's reasoned assessment of what was humane. "I think she doesn't want to lose her moonlighting job," she said.

The transfusion finished, the doctor talked more to the family. They agreed not to feed her or push anything else into her overleveraged body and add to an unbecoming death.

"She will probably pass tonight," Lampert said to me. "First, she'll move upstairs to a room. It's better. No one wants to die in the emergency room. It's calmer up there. No people all around, watching you die."

Less than an hour later, still waiting for a room, she took her last breath and died in the emergency room.

Nurses see their patients heal and become themselves again. But no matter medicine's magic, some patients don't. Nurses get reminded constantly that life goes away. After all, every twelve seconds someone dies somewhere in the country. As gets said, those who come to the ER wind up with one of three outcomes: home, admission, or heaven.

Still, death is difficult for nurses. Seeing it makes them think about life. One nurse told me, "The first time someone died I wasn't prepared. It felt sacred being in the room with him. I felt privileged being in the room, holding his hand until he was no longer alive." In her years as a nurse, Lampert has seen uncounted deaths: patients going through their final struggles and losing to heart attacks and strokes and pneumonia and simple old age.

The first death came almost at once. A man in his seventies, a dialysis patient, found unresponsive in his room. The date remains crystal clear and is fixed in her memory for one reason. It occurred just a few months after she started as a nurse. "I remember it because it happened on seven-eleven," she said. "It was Slurpee Day, when you can get free Slurpees at 7-Eleven, and my friend, another nurse, had gone to get Slurpees for us."

An atrophied man arrived not long after the transfusion woman. Pneumonia. Sepsis. Respiratory issues. Ninety-four. His son was an anesthesiologist. The patient knew the hard facts of bodies that continued only with mechanical help, understood that lives are stories that have a finish. He was DNR. He would be admitted and die.

Two deaths, one shift. Lampert acknowledged that reality without much outward display of emotion. "It's one of the common things people do in hospitals," she said. "They die."

Being too sensitive to the fact that lives end interferes with a nurse's ability to do her job. Some nurses feel a thudding guilt when they lose a patient, even if they know nothing plausible could have prevented the outcome. Their goal is to keep people alive. Lampert never feels guilt, but each death is emotional for her. "I don't think I've ever felt it was my fault or that I could have done something different," she told me. "Do I get emotional? Absolutely. With every patient, it's a life. It's more of a comfort when you feel a patient is in a better place, whatever that means."

The hardest deaths are the ones that go past any understanding. "We had a nineteen-year-old girl a couple of years ago with a lot of bad allergies," Lampert said. "She was brought in after her parents found her unresponsive and by then there was nothing we could do. Watching her mother throw herself on her daughter's body was horrible to see. There was a baby who came in. The father had been with the baby on the couch, giving his tired wife a break, and he fell asleep and rolled over and suffocated the baby. How do you forget that?"

With all deaths, nurses follow a protocol. "If the family is coming to see them, you don't want them covered with blood or vomit," Lampert said. "You want them to look as peaceful as possible." They remove all tubes, unless the body is going to the medical examiner, then they remain.

The techs normally ready the corpse for the morgue, though nurses sometimes do it. Lampert has on occasion. "You tie the feet, tie the hands, the eyes must be shut," she said. "You take off all the jewelry. Put on a toe tag. Then you fit them into a body bag."

Every once in a while, something staggering and ungraspable happens. A child dies for no comprehendible reason. They weren't in an automobile accident or trapped in a fire, they weren't born with a dreaded disease. They just seemed to die when God wasn't looking.

They brought the boy in shortly after nine in the morning. He was already in cardiac arrest. His parents had thought that he had a simple stomachache, but he worsened. Three years old.

A team mobilized and did their work as best as it could be done. The team labored over him for an hour and a half. He couldn't be saved. The suspicion was that an internal hernia might have strangled his bowel, but that verdict would have to wait. The body had to go to the chief medical examiner's office, which investigates unexpected deaths. The police had been in the ER, watched it all unfold. They would have to talk to the parents when the moment was right, visit the home.

The pain for the parents was unimaginable. A thick pall as well dropped over the entire ER. A tiny life had been taken in their room and it crushed them. "Children aren't supposed to die," Fogarty told me. "It's very hard to rationalize. We had to pull each other through the day." Brokenhearted people went around checking on each other—again and again. "I don't think I've ever been hugged so many times," Fogarty said.

The Nineteenth Precinct, where the officers were from, were so impressed by the efforts of the ER that the next day they sent over three dozen doughnuts. The ER staff joked about it: what, the police sending doughnuts rather than receiving them? But they were touched by the unusual gesture.

On Monday mornings, there is always a huddle meeting open to the entire hospital at which caring moments are spoken of, initiatives presented. At the next week's gathering, the hospital's executive director and medical director recounted the tragic incident, told about the efforts of the ER to try to save him, told about the doughnuts.

The medical director called it "one of the most powerful moments of teamwork I've ever seen."

The executive director said: "We do this every day, and there are sad events every day and there are dramatic moments every day. So thank the whole ER for this caring moment."

Everyone in the room applauded the ER.

For weeks afterward, the rattled nurses still spoke about the death. Lampert was off when it happened, but fellow nurses texted her and she felt distraught, wondering if she ought to come in and share the pain with her colleagues.

Her next shift, she was talking with fellow nurses at the nurses' station. "I went to class the next day," she said. "I don't even remember what I learned. I checked out."

Another nurse said, "My father was asking me about it that night. I didn't want to talk about it. I said I can't. I just can't."

Lampert said, "I mean, I have a three-year-old nephew. He gets stomachaches. This can't happen. It was just so horrible, so absolutely horrible."

12

The break room was located off the hallway just beyond
the south side. It had an inviting scruffiness. The trap-
pings were spare and plain. A couch and a few chairs, a TV
mounted on the wall were the rough amenities. A long coun-
ter held a microwave and coffee maker, a communal refrigerator adjacent to it. Rows of small lockers were available for
stowing belongings. It was a place to come up for oxygen.
Here, in its cyclic rhythms, nurses, doctors, and fellow staff
wolfed down meals, read, brooded, answered text messages,
watched TV, slowed racing heart rates, recharged frazzled
brains, chewed over subjects of mutual interest not necessarily of any great profundity and, in their most honored diver-
sion, vented. It's where the crankiness of their work spit out,
where transgressions small and large poured into the open.

Lampert typically uses her breaks to eat, meet a friend,
or just mellow out elsewhere. Often, she unwinds by taking
a walk alone, to think about things. Now and again, she'll
settle down in the break room and, in broadcasting her views,

be as introspective and opinionated as anyone else. But it isn't her favorite sanctuary. "It gets kind of rowdy in there," she said. "People start venting about something that happened on their shift. It'll go on for like three days. Of course, I vent too."

Amid the loose bonhomie and shared ethos of the room, they vent about mean patients. They vent about fellow nurses. They vent about doctors. They vent about hospital procedures. They vent about having too much to do in too little time. Lampert said, "You also vent about your personal life. You work so many hours and so your colleagues are your second family. They know more about you than your own family. It's a very overstimulating job, so you have to release your emotions. Nurses are human. Patients seem to forget that."

Lampert, for instance, loves nursing, except those times when she doesn't. She has a primal aversion to cleaning feces-strewn messes and cleaning sores, especially if they are rampant: "They're gross." Nursing is, at times, gross. One afternoon, a man with a penurious look and not much wrong with him came in. His body emitted a putrid odor that made the whole ER smell, and the nurses insisted he take an immediate shower. Welcome to nursing.

And everyone grumbles about a problem-riddled and wasteful health care system, the hubris of insurers. "It's a broken system," is Lampert's view. "The way that people use the emergency room. They're very misinformed. It's customer service. We have to treat every patient well or they can go elsewhere. I don't believe in socialized medicine. But there's a lot of red tape. There are a lot of steps for people to navigate health care. There's a shortage of primary care doctors because most doctors specialize—that's where the money is. That's a problem."

A subject getting good mileage one afternoon among the nurses milling in the break room was the infuriating young guy with the tumult of curly hair. He presented at the triage desk with no urgent need. He did suffer from sickle cell anemia and mentioned vague pain. He came almost weekly. His true motive, the nurses believed, was larceny. He had history. On a previous occasion, he had stolen a cell phone. Once, he struck the cop assigned to the ER. Rather than stay in his assigned location, he obstinately circled the room, asking a barrage of miscellaneous questions. Laconic in disposition, he had vast time in which to be indefensibly annoying. Lampert said, "He'll go, 'Can I have a glass of water?' 'Can I have a ginger ale with ice?' No. Literally, no!" He was a prominent example of what some nurses classify a PITA (pain in the ass). His presence this day was once again having an aggregate effect on the nerves of the nurses.

It being a regular Monday, the ER was in high gear, everything spinning fast. There were sixty-six patients, seven more waiting outside. In the beds were a pulmonary embolism, an unable to walk, a numbness in the left cheek, an anemia thrombocytopenia, a fall, a shortness of breath, a flank pain, a cellulitis of left lower extremity. There were a few stroke codes. A couple of suicidals. There was a middle-aged woman who had watched in horror as a father cradling his five-year-old daughter jumped in front of a subway. He was killed, the daughter miraculously survived. The witness was traumatized. There was a stone-cold drunk, a self-centered Russian guy scooped up off the street by paramedics. He was pretty loosened up and he told Lampert, "I think I'm dead." She told him, "You look very alive to me." The paramedic who brought him in said, "What he needs is a dog, something to pet." Lampert pointed out that they didn't prescribe dogs there. A few gallons of coffee might help. Lampert asked the tipsy man how tall he was. He estimated 180 meters—that would mean that he was 590 feet tall. For his wardrobe, he was handed a yellow robe that signaled that he was inebriated, and installed in the hallway to sober up.

Lampert, who was the charge nurse, had been lamenting, "We've got about seventy thousand patients today." She also suggested at one point, "Can we put up a sign that says we're closed for business?"

Thus, who needed the wandering man?

He created the day's talked-about drama when, confirming his reputation, he again swiped a nurse's cell phone. He brazenly demanded forty dollars to tell where it was. A security guard ponied up twenty dollars of the extortion money; the nurse gave him the balance. He revealed that he had stashed the phone in the garbage in the bathroom. Once it was retrieved, security forced him to return the money and kicked him out. The emergency in this case was the need to expel him.

The nurse assigned to him plopped down in a corner of the break room, a stricken look on her face. There was a broody air to the room. Annoying patients wedge their way into a nurse's consciousness and can ruin their shift. "I literally have chest pains," she said. "I'm palpitating."

Lampert said, "I can imagine. I know what you're going through. I'm mad too."

"You know, I would rather have someone having a heart attack than someone like that," the other nurse said.

"I know. I would definitely rather have someone really sick."

"It's just so emotionally draining, I can't stand it."

Lampert said, "It's awful, the stress of it. I mean, I'm feeling it too."

The face of the shaken nurse washed empty. She was exhausted and her day had hours to go. She said, "I need to go walk. First a cupcake."

One pleasantry in the break room this day was Lampert's annual bake sale, "Sweets For Life." She had lugged in several big boxes stuffed with goodies she had baked: cinnamon buns, cupcakes, cookies, pumpkin muffins. They were available for sale to the staff, all proceeds funneling to a favorite charity of Lampert's called Chai Lifeline. It sponsored programs and services to help children with life-threatening illnesses. Every November, Lampert also runs in their fundraising race in Las Vegas.

Lampert likes to bake and finds it therapeutic. A few years ago, she had made a cake for a manager celebrating being cancer-free. Every year at the hospital, nurses who earn health care–related degrees hold a celebration, and Lampert bakes cakes for that. And now the dollars were flowing in for the bake sale, the staff hungrily snapping up the sweets and spoiling their upcoming lunches. I bought a muffin.

It being Monday, another popular conversation-starter was the Work Note Phenomenon. Nurses can reliably expect a certain number of Monday arrivals with assorted mythical complaints and one real one: they don't want to go to work.

A nurse said, "They'll say they hadn't been feeling well for several days and then, oddly enough, come in Sunday night or Monday morning to get a work note."

A work note is a signed note from a nurse or doctor confirming that the person had been at the emergency room, thus their necessary absence from their job. A get-out-of-work-free card.

One nurse said, "Sometimes if it doesn't seem like there is anything particularly wrong with them, I'll go ahead and ask them, 'Are you here for a work note?' And sometimes they'll actually say yes."

Lampert said, "We do appreciate the honesty."

They still get the note.

Lampert rubbed her neck. "My neck is so bad," she said. "It's like popcorn. When I'm driving, I get tingling in my fingers."

Being a nurse assaults the body. Especially the back. Having a bad back is pretty much a given. Shoulder injuries are commonplace. Knee pain. Hospital patients tend to be older, sicker, and heavier than ever (there are three-hundred-pound patients; there are five-hundred-pound patients). Nurses must routinely move and reposition them. Hospitals have floor and ceiling mechanical lifts, some of which can manage up to a thousand pounds. But nurses often do without them because there simply isn't time, especially in the ER, or because they're in use elsewhere. Nurses are taught appropriate body mechanics for lifting, but studies suggest these don't help much in preventing injuries. One estimate has it that the average nurse in a hospital or nursing home lifts 1.8 tons per shift.

Nurses are bending all the time. They are bending to insert IVs and bending to draw blood and bending to take vital signs. It puts strain on their bodies. Nurses are reminded to raise the bed when they're doing these things, so they don't have to bend as often. Lampert's back is all right. She works out regularly to try to keep it that way. It's her neck that continues to ache.

Sore feet are another common complaint. Like hairdressers and chefs, nurses are constantly on their feet. I read a study that concluded that a typical nurse walks something like four to five miles every shift. Watching Lampert endlessly ramble through the ER, I had difficulty believing it was that little. All the walking and standing puts inordinate stress on joints and muscles. Varicose veins are commonplace. Many nurses address this by wearing compression socks and sneakers or clogs.

No matter what precautions nurses take, injuries mount up. I learned of nurses who had to have back operations at premature ages, nurses who had to have foot surgery. The Bureau of Labor Statistics reports that nurses suffer among the most frequent workplace injuries of all professions. Fractures, strains, sprains, cuts. In terms of risk to their bodies, their jobs rival construction work.

Exposed to so much illness and germs on a daily basis, nurses are susceptible to getting sick themselves. That seems to always happen when they begin their careers. Long enough on the job, they build up powerful immune systems. "New nurses always get sick," Lampert told me. "Veteran nurses don't. It's a known thing with new nurses. When I started out, I would have the once a year flu-like thing. I trucked through it and came to work anyway."

After twelve hours of tending to ailing bodies, Lampert needs to wipe the day from her brain and restore her equilibrium. Nursing is physical labor and it's emotional labor. The work assails the body and it peals at the heart. When you leave your shift, it takes time for the ER to release its hold. As Irene Macyk put it, "It drains your empathy bank. A lot of nurses feel caregiver distress."

When that happens, nurses find themselves becoming more tired, less animated, less social, wrapped up in their own misery.

Sometimes they see especially awful things on the job—the death of a patient they had become close to, the unpredicted death of a colleague. The hospital has a Code Lavender that it calls to comfort a team when something like this happens, which is maybe once a month. Staffers come with a convenience cart loaded with chocolates, squeeze balls, and lavender, and sit down to talk it out.

Nurses come to the work to care, but caring too much can take too much from a nurse. One study of Midwestern nurses found that those who cared the most were the ones most likely to burn out.

Earlier that day when I greeted Lampert, she was far from her cheery self. "I can't even believe how tired I am," she said. "I came home last night and I had to study and there was no time. I may cry today I'm so tired." She spent her first break sleeping.

The mounting complexities of nursing figure into why studies suggest that a quarter to a third of nurses leave their first job within two years.

Lampert and her fellow nurses do laugh a lot. Yes, you can laugh in the emergency room. The ER is a serious, anxiety-suffused place of suffering. Among its contradictions, though, is that those who work there need to cut loose and laugh. Nurses even laugh at things that would not be remotely funny to other people. Levity affords them an outlet and a shield against the continuous anguish that they witness.

"It's part of dealing with stress and it's just part of who we are," Lampert told me. "In the ER you see the worst of society and the best of society and the strangest of society."

One afternoon, between demands on their time, Lampert and several other nurses were discussing how they regularly crack up over nurse and medical humor memes, hundreds of which skitter across the internet and get at the underbelly of nursing: memenurseofficial, rnratchet, nurselifern, codebluememes. The latter is a particular favorite. They ritually cluck over the latest postings, hearing echoes of their own experiences. It's a trenchant Instagram and Twitter rendering from a male Chicago ER nurse, who identifies himself by writing, "When I'm not saving lives with turkey sandwiches, I'm making memes on IG/FB."

Some samples:

Why did you become a nurse?
  What I say: I wanted to help people and make a difference in their lives
  What I think: I wanted to wear pajamas at work

The speed of light is approximately 300,000 km per second Or about as fast as it takes for your patient to hit the call button when you sit down at the nurses station

What do you do for a living?
  Nurse: I professionally apologize for things outside of my control

So Netflix has a new show called Awake where contestants stay awake for 24 hours then stumble through a variety of memory and reflex challenges to win a million dollar grand prize. I'm a night-shift nurse. I'll take my million in tens and twenties please.

Patients get mad for two reasons:
   1. For everything
   2. For nothing

As a single night-shift nurse, what I'm really looking for on dating apps: Someone who's available to go on a date at 9 a.m. on weekdays.

"We send these back and forth among us all the time," Lampert said. "They're all totally accurate."

One of the other nurses said, "They validate our feelings."

Another source of humor are the surreal are-you-kidding-me complaints of arriving patients in the ER. Ones that have nurses rolling their eyes deepest into their sockets. Impromptu, one of the nurses fished out her phone and swiped through it to reveal some of her laughable favorites:

"I'm just trying to maintain my general health."

"I have a sore throat after eating cake."

"I played basketball seventeen years ago and it still hurts."

"I passed out while sleeping."

Lampert showed me one on her phone: "Wind blowing door open and hitting my face."

Another nurse topped that: "I had one where she said that her pinkies were too long." Yes, it had arisen in the woman's mind that she should speed to the emergency room because she preferred shorter pinkies.

One day a man presented, his complaint a stab wound. When did this happen? Thirteen years ago. Why was he here now? To check if it was still all right.

One of the nurses piped up to promote her all-time favorite, a man who, when asked his complaint, gave the concise answer that it was none of the nurse's business, injecting an expletive to underscore his position.

When I asked Lampert how, besides humor, she managed the emotional strain of her shifts, she said, "I try to disconnect when I'm out of work. I literally have days where I just fall off the map. Go to Barnes & Noble. Go to the mall. Not interact with other people. After a twelve-hour shift, I don't want to talk to anybody. You've been talking to people for twelve hours. You don't want to hear your own voice. And I don't want to hear anyone else's complaints. That's all you've heard all day. One of the challenges of being a nurse is everyone wants to know about something. When you're a nurse, you're everybody's nurse. You get pictures of things on your phone. Like you get pictures of rashes. What do you think this is? Should I be nervous about this? Do I have cancer? Am I dying? After a shift, what I do is I get in my car and turn on my music. Country music—I love any kind of country music. I listen and disconnect. That's why I like to drive. After being here all day, I like the space. I don't have to share the train with my patients. There are no patients. I'm the only one in this vicinity and it's good."

13

Nurses are witches. Nurses are bimbos. Nurses are sex objects. Nurses do nothing, doctors do everything. This is what you see on TV and in movies, read in books. Doctors are glamorized, nurses deglamorized.

Nurses bristle at the now expected portrayals of themselves in popular culture. They are not—or at least few of them are—Nurse Ratched ("Big Nurse"), the glacial, heartless tyrant in *One Flew Over the Cuckoo's Nest*. They are not Sairey Gamp, the drunken and monstrous nurse in Charles Dickens's *The Life and Adventures of Martin Chuzzlewit*. Medical TV shows depict them as condescended to by hubristic doctors, sex options, background furniture. They're shown as low-skilled and unambitious—otherwise, they would have become doctors. That is, if they include them at all. Stereotypes thus linger and flourish and insult.

"We have a terrible image," Cathy Fogarty told me. "People don't know what nurses do. They're seen as either sex symbols or they don't exist. What they are, are miracle workers."

She brought up an incident several years before when Joy Behar, one of the hosts of *The View*, was discussing a Miss America contestant who had been a nurse and appeared in the talent portion of the contest wearing scrubs and a stethoscope around her neck. Behar wondered why she had on a *doctor's* stethoscope.

"It's an insult grounded in ignorance," Fogarty said. "I mean, doctors borrow our stethoscopes, because they'll be without one. Nurses always have stethoscopes. They are *their* stethoscope."

Thousands of infuriated nurses attacked on twitter. Behar apologized on air, admitting she "didn't know what the hell [she] was talking about."

Fogarty mentioned another cutting remark from an episode of *Grey's Anatomy*, when a doctor advised an intern, "Be nice to the nurses, because it's always someone's birthday and they always have cake."

When I asked Irene Macyk about nurses in popular culture, she said: "I'm distressed by the portrayal of the nurse. In the hospital TV shows, you hardly ever see a nurse. You would think the doctor does everything. We're underrepresented. Then there was *Nurse Jackie*, which was a complete misrepresentation of nursing. I don't remember a movie where a nurse was portrayed. They just pass by in hospital scenes."

Nurse Jackie was a fictional cable-TV series focused on

Jackie Peyton, an emergency room nurse at a New York hospital addicted to prescription painkillers. She was, as well, hampered by a messy personal life. She stole to feed her drug habit and freely bent hospital rules.

The series did, however, show nurses doing worthwhile things. All too often in TV hospitals, nurses don't seem to have been invented yet. Studies reveal that in health-care articles in the media, nurses are rarely quoted. It's always doctors.

Lampert said, "In the TV shows, the nurses are very silent. In *Grey's Anatomy*, nurses don't exist. But I still love *Grey's Anatomy*. It doesn't bother me. It's fantasy. I never saw *Nurse Jackie*, but I know nurses hated it. Nurses have to represent who they are. We don't need TV shows to do it."

Tuesday, and Lampert was assigned to Zone One. She had inherited one patient from the night side, a short, bouncy woman who had fallen at home, hurting her ankle, then slipped again that morning in the bathroom. She also had lung cancer. She was waiting to be steered to X-ray.

Lampert went to greet her: "Hi, I'm Hadassah, I'm your nurse. I'm taking over for the night shift. How are you feeling?"

"Fine," the woman said. Her husband, in a Hawaiian shirt and jeans, sat beside her, nodded in agreement.

"Any pain now?" Lampert asked.

"Not right now."

"Well, you let me know if you have any."

"I will. Thank you."

In the next bed, a man was muttering, "I'm eighty years old. All sorts of things go wrong with me. For god's sake, I'm eighty years old."

As a gurney clanged past, Lampert sat down at a nearby terminal. Yesterday had been Labor Day, which she had also worked. "It was nice," she said. "I don't think we went over nineteen patients. Holidays can go either way. Be really quiet, or you get really sick people."

Another nurse slid into the chair next to Lampert. Lampert had just returned from vacation. She went to Texas for a few days and otherwise relaxed at home. Her colleague asked how it was.

"It was nice to get away from work and school and do nothing," she said. "Tomorrow's the first day back at school."

Lampert began graduate school at Rutgers two years ago and had two years left.

Her fellow nurse asked her how it was going. Lampert told her that the third year was mainly clinicals. "You're hands-on," she said. "I'll be in a no-insurance clinic in Newark. There will be a preceptor, but I'll be doing things. It will be more diagnostic, and I'll prescribe and decide what meds they need. It's a very scary transition."

The other nurse said, "In the ER, you anticipate and assist."

"But to prescribe and be the final word, it's a big jump," Lampert said. "It's exciting, but it's scary. I've seen it a lot. You know theoretically what to do. But you've never done it. You do central lines and intubation and suturing."

"It's so scary," the other nurse said.

Lampert said, "You have to fake it until you make it. Like the first time I had to give an insulin shot as a nurse, I was terrified. I was literally shaking. It's like the tiniest needle imaginable. It's nothing. Like what was I going to do—explode the arm? I had to pretend that I was so calm. You fake it until you make it."

The other nurse said, "The first time I put an IV in, I couldn't hear. I was falling over, about to faint. I was sweating unbelievably. My sweat was puddling on the floor."

"It's crazy," Lampert said. "The first time I had to do an IV, the preceptor said, have you done this before? Oh yeah, I said, a hundred times."

She fetched food for a woman. She administered some medicine. Then she went to discharge the woman who had fallen twice. Lampert brought the paperwork with instructions and went over them with her: the need to put a cold compress on the bruised area, to get rest. The woman said, yes, yes, yes.

Lampert said, "It sounds like you've got everything under control."

The woman's husband said, "Yes, we've been here many times."

"How are you with the internet?" Lampert asked him.

"Not good. I leave that to her."

Lampert swiveled to the woman and said, "I'm going to show you how to create a patient portal. You can call up all your labs and everything."

Once she had finished doing that, she said, "Anything else I can do for you today?"

The husband said, "No, I just hope you have a good life."

"I like that answer," Lampert said.

Once they had left, Lampert said to me, "That's the sort of patient you want to have. Upbeat, pleasant, grateful. And she's really sick with cancer. And a dialysis patient."

She nodded at another bed, where a young man was lying. "And then you have this guy—young, homeless, doesn't take care of himself. Nothing actually wrong with him. You can predict how it's going to go. When I went over to say you're going to be discharged, he was like, 'I'm dizzy. Can I see a neurologist?' And he has been here for like five hours. He's been walking around, taking in the scenery. All part of the job. You have to stay human."

She attended to a new arrival. He was a man in his nineties. Trimmed beard. Square face with sleepy eyes.

"Hi, I'm Hadassah, I'm going to be taking care of you. So what's going on today?"

"Everything's going wrong."

"Everything's going wrong. So how can we make it right?"

"I need a magician."

"You've been urinating too much?"

"Not enough. Different colors."

"What colors?"

"Some's yellow. Reddish brown. At the end of the day, turns black."

"And how long has this been going on for?"

"About a week."

"Any fever? Chills?"

"No."

"Any pain?"

"No."

"Has this ever happened before?"

"No."

"You've been treated for your prostate?"

"Yes. I was treated. I still have the prostate."

Lampert tried inserting an IV. It was difficult. He said it's always been difficult.

"There we go. Done."

"You're a magician," the man said with a crinkly grin. "What's your name?"

"Hadassah. You like that name?"

"I've never heard that name."

"Well, there's a first time for everything. Are you having any pain now?"

"No."

"I'm going to press on your stomach."

"Feels good," he said.

She listened to his breathing: "Take deep breaths for me."

She had him sit forward and listened. She said, "So we're going to send down for blood work. Any questions?"

"Nope."

"Okay, I'll come see you soon."

As she updated his chart, she said, "I love older, with-it patients. They're so wonderful. They're like a testament to humanity. He's ninety-two and he's a functioning, with-it person. It gives you hope."

She moved to bed 20. Middle-aged woman with straight dark hair wearing a lot of jewelry.

"Hi, I'm Hadassah, I'm a nurse here. What seems to be the problem?"

"My eye is swollen."

"When did this happen?"

"I noticed it about a week and a half ago. But it seemed worse this morning."

"Have you seen your doctor?"

"No, I just came here."

"It doesn't look that bad to me. But you're here and we'll check it out."

"I appreciate that. I want to be well."

"Any medical problems?"

"No. I don't know if the eye comes from the henna. I dye my hair and I can't use the dye, so I put the henna in."

"When did you put in the henna?"

"Two weeks ago."

"I don't think that would do it. Have you used it before?"

"Always. Never had a problem."

"Well, you're here. We'll have it checked out."

Doing her chart, Lampert told me, "That patient is a gift for me."

Why?

"Because I don't have to do anything. Just be reassuring. The eye is not going to fall out. She is not sick from a hair treatment."

Late morning, gloom outside. Lampert ducked into a Sepsis Task Force meeting. She volunteered for several hospital committees, to involve herself deeper in hospital affairs and broaden her knowledge.

The meeting was in a generously cooled conference room on the fourth floor. Arrayed around an oblong table were six participants—doctors, nurses, data analysts, a pharmacist. The task force was charged with examining how well the hospital was doing in addressing sepsis and suggesting ways to improve.

Sepsis is a huge issue for all hospitals, being a leading cause of death and a major reason why patients get readmitted. Every 3.5 seconds, someone in the world dies from sepsis, which occurs when the body has an overwhelming reaction to an infection. Sepsis mortality increases 8 percent for every hour that sepsis is delayed. If not treated swiftly, the result can be tissue damage, organ failure, and death. An important role of nurses is to recognize the symptoms of sepsis—factors like a high heart rate, fever, shivering, confusion, shortness of breath, clammy skin, extreme pain—and call a Code Sepsis.

At Lenox Hill, a Code Sepsis is called around once a day during summer months but perhaps ten times a day during the winter, flu season.

A doctor led the task force discussion. She opened the meeting by reviewing the latest metrics. On the whole, the numbers were good. They examined things like initial lactate collection and blood culture collection before antibiotic administration.

As she listened, Lampert ate her lunch, which she had brought with her from home in a plastic container.

One issue was that there had been a decrease in the number of Code Sepsis being called, as well as a decrease in the completion of the sepsis Green Sheet (a record of the sepsis activity for the hospital's internal use). It was not entirely clear what this signified, but the task force didn't believe there was less sepsis, or sepsis that was going untreated, but rather that cases weren't always being formally documented for the hospital's review.

Lampert said, "The biggest challenge is when there are so many patients. When there are constant upgrades. There shouldn't be an issue when we're not that busy."

The doctor wondered whether fewer sepsis codes were being called because the ER didn't have sufficient resources.

The data analyst asked, "Do you think you need two nurses for a Code Sepsis?"

Lampert said, "Yes, you do."

One of the other nurses said, "So let's reinforce calling it. It's going to get busy. Flu season is about to start."

There was a layer of excitement when the data analyst said, "So September is Sepsis Awareness Month. We're going to have a game where the nurse who turns in the most sepsis Green Sheets will win a prize. You'll get a point for each sheet and at the end of the month the nurse with the most points will get a fifty-dollar gift card. And each discipline gets a gift card. The doctor gets one. The tech gets one."

The doctor leading the group said, "We'll start it on the first Wednesday of September. That's the fourth."

The data analyst piped up: "There will be other games, like if you get answers to questions, you'll get movie tickets."

The doctor said, "Or you'll get a hat. If you get three out of three questions, you'll get movie tickets. We'll do that every Wednesday. We're also thinking goodies. Like cupcakes."

Lampert said, "I'll bake something."

The doctor said, "That's great, Hadassah."

Lampert said, "What number? Fifty?"

"Fifty would be great."

14

Often in recent decades, there haven't been enough nurses. Media dispatches in the 1980s and into the early 2000s told of troubling shortages, with there being as many as 75,000 to 125,000 openings for nurses without candidates to fill them. Projections were that shortfalls would worsen as the over one million nurses in the Baby Boomer generation retired. The government warned of a shortage of eight hundred thousand nurses by 2020, which would paralyze the health care system.

Worried about that frightening prospect, the government and private companies, most notably Johnson & Johnson, launched elaborate campaigns to promote nursing. Johnson & Johnson did things like create a group of cartoon nurses known as the Nursing Gang that engaged in games on a DVD that school nurses gave out to preteens. Nursing schools became more innovative and accommodating, including offering the chance to study nursing online. The federal government made loans for nursing students available.

All this stimulated interest in nursing. Millennials, to a surprising degree, flocked to the field. The tragedy of 9/11, which spurred many people to select more meaningful careers, galvanized a good number of those in their thirties and forties to change careers and become nurses.

"Now we feel we will be able to replace the more than one million Baby Boom nurses who will have retired by 2030, and add to that," said Peter Buerhaus, a professor in the College of Nursing at Montana State University and an expert on the nursing workforce.

The Labor Department is projecting continued growth in demand, but possibly a surplus of nurses by 2030. Buerhaus, though, is skeptical. "Medicaid expansion is growing demand," he said. "The mental health crisis is growing demand. A shortage of primary care physicians is growing demand. Just the aging population is growing demand. So we've got a lot of fuel growing the demand for nurses."

Nursing is a decent-paying profession, with a median salary for registered nurses of about $70,000, well above the income for all professions. (For licensed practical nurses, the median is about $46,000, while for advanced practice nurses it's $114,000.) One attraction is the option of per diem jobs and overtime. Shifts exist at other hospitals, doctor offices, or urgent care centers. This opportunity for extra income helps with credit card bills that veer out of control or for vacation funds or "treat yourself money." On a number of occasions, I heard the Lenox Hill nurses swap information on shift opportunities, places where the census is light and patients tend to be younger and the presenting conditions more stomachaches than strokes. Some nurses moonlight by giving flu shots at health fairs. Some do home infusion visits. If someone is mightily hungover or seriously jet lagged or otherwise too exhausted to face the day and needs to be hydrated or get antibiotics administered intravenously at home or their hotel, they can call a service and a nurse will stop by. Mobile hydration services like The I.V. Doc, dubbed by some the "Uber of Hangovers," offer these house calls (there's also an I.V. Doc gift card available if you're "looking for the perfect gift"). Lampert told me she was contemplating doing home infusion. Easy money—$75 to $100 a visit plus travel expenses.

Many nurses become nurses after doing something else. One of the ER nurses at Lenox Hill told me that she began her career at a hedge fund, found no passion for the dedicated pursuit of money and became a nurse. A male nurse at a different hospital worked at a library, then taught school before moving to nursing. Other nurses become nurses because early exposure to nursing made a positive impression. Another of Lampert's colleagues got strep throat repeatedly as a child, was in and out of the hospital. She came to know many nurses. They treated her wonderfully and their kindness was imprinted on her. She became one of them.

More men continue to enter the profession, though 90 percent of nurses are women. As with doctors, the geographical distribution of nurses is skewed. Metropolitan areas, for the most part, have a sufficient pool. On the other hand, the influx is sorely inadequate in many rural areas with thin populations. That problem has been around forever, and persists.

The average age of a nurse is about fifty, and more than a million nurses are fifty and older. "One interesting thing going on is we're halfway through the retirement of the nurses from the Baby Boom generation," Buerhaus said. "We will replace them, but we will replace them with nurses with limited experience. I'm saying goodbye to Martha, but I'm going to need two people to replace her. So we're looking at a qualitative shortage."

Expectations are that nursing employment will continue to migrate to outpatient clinics, surgical centers, and home care positions, in keeping with health care trends. But it's a slow migration. As demand for health care continues to accelerate, more nurses are expected to be involved in primary care and assume functions that were customarily the sole province of doctors. Many young nurses work for a while in hospitals, then return for advanced degrees and become nurse practitioners. "We estimate that it's taking eighty thousand nurses out of hospitals," Buerhaus said. "For some hospitals, this is a quantitative problem."

Lenox Hill and two of its sister locations together hire about a hundred and fifty nurses a year. Cathy Fogarty told me that there are plenty of applicants, but it's hard to find the "right" nurses. "They have to be clinically excellent," she said. "They have to have kindness and compassion and be team players. Nursing is a team activity. You have to be open to change. Things change every day. Nursing is always changing. Patients are different every day."

Irene Macyk told me that for every position there are around seventy applicants. Out of those, six make it to an interview, and one gets hired.

Talking about her own criteria, she told me: "I want you to come in because you really care about the patient. I'm looking for someone who is excited, who asks the why. I'm a bit of a hiring snob."

"How do you know someone cares?" I asked her.

"You can tell by the way they make eye contact. You can tell by the way they tell stories if it's a genuine story. I'll ask you to tell a time that you've had a personal struggle and how you overcame it. To tell about a time you were triumphant. It'll tell by how you relate interpersonally. If someone sits here and they won't make eye contact and they give all the chic answers, that's not who I want."

15

The phone buzzed.

Lampert answered it. A discharged patient had lost his backpack, was it there? "One moment," Lampert said. She hunted around, looked here, looked there. "I don't see a backpack," she said.

Lampert was charge nurse. In that role, overlord of the ER, she was enmeshed in everything that went on, including misplaced possessions. Above all, she had to assign patients to beds and to nurses, directing the flow of the room. She had to address maintenance issues if, say, a heart monitor was broken, or the ER was short blood-pressure cuffs. Once, she faced a ceiling leak. She coordinated breaks for the nurses and techs. She did periodic "rounds," circling the entire ER to see if everything was humming.

During days when she was the charge nurse, I'd seen her do ambulance triage when multiple arrivals showed up, strip beds once patients had been discharged, fetch a blanket, steer a patient to the bathroom, bring an uncomfortable man an extra pillow, deliver heat packs for someone's back, roll a bed in, whatever needed doing when everyone was beleaguered. All of this, nursing too.

Sitting staunchly at her post, Lampert spent the bulk of her time staring contemplatively at the "board" on the screen before her. It listed the active patients in the ER, along with pertinent details. Age, chief complaint, acuity level, their bed location, assigned nurse, attending doctor, whether they needed labs, urine sample, CAT scan, X-ray, and so on.

Another monitor in easy view gave the status of the heart monitors in all the beds. Taped to the monitor was a chart on measles ("Know what to look for and how to respond") and a flyer for a missing person with dementia and a heart condition, last spotted five days ago.

"Here, you have to know everything," Lampert told me. "You have to know the answer to everything. If you don't know it, you better find out. There are a lot of phone calls, too. In this role, it's not just patient care. It's also customer service."

Of course, no nurse or doctor knows everything. When something unfamiliar arises—a set of symptoms or medication—Lampert trawls through one of two favored medical websites used by nurses and doctors alike: Medscape and UpToDate. "How to treat guidelines for different conditions are always changing, so you look them up," she said. "I use these almost daily. Especially now that I'm in school to be a nurse practitioner, I am even more inclined to look things up. I like to know the reason why we do things."

In the constant flux, Lampert was expertly directing traffic, putting a chest pain in bed 3, a mover who had a refrigerator fall on him in bed 9. She got a hungry guy a peanut butter and jelly sandwich. She got a woman an extra pillow. She put an IV in a husky, middle-aged man complaining of fever and pain in his groin. He winced as she gingerly inserted the needle, kicked his feet up and down. She told him, "You should know I'm the biggest baby with a needle. I can give them, but when it comes to me, it's a different story."

Before long, the place was saturated and a new arrival needed to be on a cardiac monitor. Lampert checked the board, ordered someone who didn't require a monitor shifted to the hall and the new patient rolled in. Musical beds. Bumper beds.

The ambulance brought in a hopelessly uncooperative patient, the sort who can exasperate nurses, make them wonder, is this really happening? Middle-aged man with arched eyebrows and dazed eyes, hair cut so short it was practically invisible. Long into a bender. His jacket was splotched with food. The paramedics had retrieved him from a nearby corner, where he was about to slide into the sewer. One of the paramedics was saying, "People were standing there in the rain videotaping it to make sure we were doing it right. As if they know what doing it right is. They think they know because they saw it on TV. No, it should be done like that. Oh really? Where'd you see that? Season four, episode eight of something or other. Thanks for your help. Thanks for telling us how to do our job."

Information was not forthcoming from the man, even his name. In what was turning into a tautological farce, he rambled on about his pursuit of the American Dream.

Paramedic: "You've got to sober up to get the American Dream."

Man: "I've been sleeping for four years. I need a job."

Paramedic: "There are plenty of jobs. Burger King. Starbucks."

Man: "I need a job for the American Dream."

Paramedic: "How about Wednesday? How about you get a job Wednesday? Now what's your birthday?"

Man: "I don't have one."

Paramedic: "Everyone has a birthday. Listen, let me explain. You're in New York City. The way it goes here, you have to provide me with a name and a birthday."

Man: "I don't remember. My head isn't working."

Paramedic: "Your head isn't working because you're drunk."

Man: "Baby, I want my American Dream."

Paramedic: "I'm not 'baby.' Address me properly. Ma'am."

This was going nowhere. Lampert came over, regarded

him for a moment, and gave it a try: "Hi, I'm Hadassah. What's your name?"

Man: "My American Dream is my American Dream. I want to go to Washington."

Lampert: "What's your name?"

Man: "I want to go to Washington."

Lampert: "I know where you want to go. What's your name?"

Man: "I want to go to Los Angeles. That's my American Dream. If not, you can kill me. I have no problem with that."

The paramedic said to Lampert: "I told him where the American Dream is. Once he sobers up, hopefully he can find it. I found it. On the way, he said he was going to work for his uncle's BP station, after he got Social Security disability. Meanwhile, he falls into a sewer with people watching and he could have had a lawsuit against the city. That's what it's come to."

Lampert said, "It's pathetic."

Paramedic: "It is. It's totally pathetic."

Lampert: "It is what it is."

The gulf between them too wide, Lampert registered him without a name. Then he got up and unceremoniously walked out.

Quitting time was almost upon her. Everything was under control. The nurses were long in their shift, much of the fire out of them, the bliss of the end of a day's work in sight. Lampert chatted with a few of them. The conversation varied, more often than not characteristically entertaining less serious matters than splenic infarctions and chronic obstructive pulmonary disease. They discussed dating issues, how their hours impinged on relationships, the offensive price of cell phones. Frowns and shakes of heads. The nurse seated next to her wondered if Lampert might like her recipe for stuffed peppers. Lampert was quick to say yes.

A nurse excitedly reported that after an extensive search she had found an apartment, a tidy duplex to share with a fellow nurse. It featured a backyard for her dog and a washer and dryer in the apartment.

"That is wild," Lampert said. "That is the biggest thing. It means you won't have to be schlepping laundry. So great!"

The nurse pulled out her phone and Lampert and the others bunched around to examine pictures of the apartment.

Lampert said, "I really want to live on a farm. I would hire a farmer, but I want to live on a farm."

"Are you being for real?" one of the other nurses said. "Like a farm with pigs and goats and wheat growing."

"No, not like that."

Lampert said to me, "This is like the witching hour. When we all go stir-crazy from being on so long."

So what do you do?

"This."

In the evolving discussion, one nurse said, "There's a cute cardiology fellow I want to set my friend up with."

The telephone rang. Lampert grabbed it, was informed that a patient was bringing a service dog.

She asked another nurse, "Can a husky be a service dog?"

"Any dog can."

"I'm not going near it."

"You're afraid of a husky."

"Well, it's a big dog."

One of the nurses arrived with a box of candy. A grateful patient had brought it by. This was excellent news. It was quickly parceled out. Take one, two—okay, five.

Appreciation from patients and their family members is always welcome. They send gooey thank-you cards. They send flowers. They send food. Lampert told me about an instance of rapport when she worked on the floors: "There was this woman who had breathing problems and was very sick and she eventually passed. She had a difficult personality. She hated her situation. You just sit down with them and get to their level, and that's what I did. The last time I saw her, she gave me a gift. A bottle of Tommy Hilfiger perfume. The most awful-smelling perfume. But it was her favorite perfume. She wrote a note with it about how I was the best nurse. I still have the perfume and note on my dresser. I'll keep it forever."

She went on: "A year-and-a-half into my ER career, the charge nurse told me I was getting a stroke upgrade. A woman twenty-seven or twenty-eight. Slurred speech. Couldn't get the words out. But she knew what was happening to her. She went in for a CAT scan. It turned out she had a massive brain tumor. It looked like it took over the whole right side of her brain. As we looked at the picture on the monitor, the doctor and I started crying. Of course, she was the nicest person. It only happens to the nicest people. We took her back from the CAT scan and she started having a seizure. We gave her anti-seizure medication. We gave her steroids. Slowly she started speaking a little better. She had a two-year-old. I went with her to get an MRI and got her up to the neurosurgery ICU. I left. The one hard thing about ER is you leave and you don't always find out what happened. You can try, but it's hard. I was on vacation for a week and when I came back a nurse told me a patient had left a letter for me. I opened the letter, and it started out, 'Hadassah, two weeks ago I was in your emergency room and it was the worst day of my life. Ten days later, the tumor is out and I'm doing better.' She gave some Biblical explanation about the name Hadassah. You know, you do what you have to do and you don't understand the impression you're having on someone. You really can make a difference. That's what nursing is. You make a difference."

She thought a moment and added one more story: "Some

patients I've known as both an inpatient and in the ER for over nine years, my whole career. One woman I had on the floors. She had pneumonia. Once when she was my patient, my sister was a senior in high school and having graduation pictures taken. My mom drove her in and on my break I went to do her makeup in the car outside. Every time I see this woman, she teases me about doing the makeup in the car. It's amazing how people remember such things. People remember the nurses. You're there all the time at the bedside. The doctor comes in for five minutes."

An important recognition Lampert received in 2018 was the Daisy Award for Extraordinary Nurses, one of nursing's most prestigious honors. It originated with the Barnes family. Their son, Patrick, died in 1999, at age thirty-three, from complications of ITP, an autoimmune disease that can trigger excessive bleeding. He was hospitalized for eight weeks, and his family was struck by the kindness of the nurses. They knew they wanted to honor their son by doing something lasting for them. They started an organization called Daisy, standing for diseases attacking the immune system, and created the Daisy Award.

Nurses can be nominated by a patient, family member, doctor, administrator, or anyone in their organization. Lampert was nominated by the widow of a man she had treated on several occasions and who died, at eighty-eight, from cancer. He came about ten times to the ER in a year. Each time something different. Pneumonia. Infection. Still, he was always in a chipper mood. Before he died, he was admitted and Lampert used to visit him. Not long afterward, his wife wrote a letter to the hospital: "Whenever we were in emergency and Hadassah was on, she was the first one greeting us with a smile and comforting my husband first and then the family. Her attention to detail and ease of making the patient comfortable was really special. Emergency duty is filled with so many things, but she makes it look easy. Her smile and confidence—two things so needed in those times—are a testament to who she is. It didn't hurt that I received a genuine hug as we were discharged!"

When it was time to present the award at a ceremony in the ER, the widow showed up to give it to Lampert. She received a pin, a certificate, and a hand-carved stone sculpture from Zimbabwe called "Healer's Touch."

One day during his illness, Patrick Barnes had no appetite and his father offered him his cinnamon roll. He found it delicious. The next day he requested another one, as well as rolls for all the nurses in the unit. When the award is presented, the nurse's department always earns a supply of cinnamon rolls. When Lampert got her award, Cinnabon sent over several boxes of rolls. The ER smelled like a bakery.

16

The woman arrived screaming. Paramedics wheeled her in from the ambulance bay. She had frizzy hair and wore a short, rumpled skirt.

"I'm in pain," she shrieked. "Please, I'm in pain."

Though in a sitting position on the stretcher, she was doubled over, her hands clutching her stomach. She was in her midforties, scrawny, her hair drawn back tight. Around her neck was a dazzling necklace.

Lampert threaded her way to her. "Hi, my name is Hadassah," she said. "I'm one of the nurses here. I'm going to put in an IV so I can give you something. When did it start?"

The EMT who brought her in said, "It started a couple of hours ago. Pain and vomiting."

"Please, please, please," the woman screamed. Her voice engulfed the emergency room.

Lampert said in a flat voice, "Lean back. I need to get the IV in. I hear that you're in pain."

"Please, please, please."

"I know. But I need to get an IV in or I can't do anything."

Lampert seemed unmoved by the woman's continuous outburst. She calmly put an IV in her arm, but without her customary display of empathy.

When she sat down to do the woman's chart, letting the cool of the room pass over her, she explained why. The woman was a conniver.

"Nothing's going on but drama," she said. "She's been here before multiple times with the same presentation. And nothing's wrong."

Another nurse said of her manufactured emotion: "She claims she's been crying for two hours and yet you can see that her face is dry."

Why was she doing it?

"Because she wants pain medication," Lampert said.

Will she get it?

"No. She'll get what's appropriate."

She was a Frequent Flyer. Every ER has its steady invasion of Frequent Flyers who add to the ER churn. These are patients who return repeatedly, sometimes days apart, commonly under false or exaggerated auspices. Many come casually, as if visiting the nail salon or the barber. They come with an angle. They're ER hustlers. Some show up again and again simply for a bed and to wheedle a couple of meals. At times, their pretext will be that they're considering throwing themselves in front of the number 6 train. Or they're hearing sinister voices. They troop from ER to ER. When they're ready to leave, they confess that they have no interest in facing the number 6 train, have heard no internal voices. Frequent Flyers also include those who do in fact need legitimate care. Often because they don't take their medicine or follow up with their doctor, if they have a doctor.

By federal law, the ER can't refuse someone, and so everyone must be seen and the real disentangled from the fake. One day, a guy came in expressing concern over a vague pain, was seen and discharged, after which he walked out, perhaps circled the block, and returned to be seen again for a vague pain. He was a Frequent Frequent Flyer. An EMT told me that some people call for ambulances so often that they know the codes the paramedics use: "Like Lenox Hill here is hospital eleven, and they'll say, take me to eleven. Or they'll say, take me to code fourteen. That's Cornell. They direct us around like we're taxi drivers."

The doctors and nurses see through these Flyers' excitable behavior and looping repetitions. Lampert's patience seems inexhaustible. But it exhausts with yet another appearance by an unnecessary Frequent Flyer. "They abuse the system," Lampert said. "They don't want to have a regular doctor.

They usually don't have an emergency. Some are very sick but most aren't. Most are repeat nuisances. They have no reason to be here."

A gimlet-eyed doctor with a high forehead stopped by to see the sobbing woman, now flat-backed on the stretcher. She was still shrieking about her pain. Patiently, he said to her, "You've had three CAT scans in the last year for the same thing. Nothing's showed up."

The woman gave a look of regret. Then she droned on: "Please, please, please."

Terse dialogue continued between doctor and patient, reaching a stalemate.

Once she abandoned her unpersuasive act, she would be discharged, and if there was anything certain, it was that she would hop back on the ER merry-go-round and reappear before long.

On a later afternoon, a woman arrived interested in some IV fluids because of dizziness. While being treated, she was on the phone nonchalantly telling someone that she would be reporting next to the NYU emergency room for a different condition, so she'd have to catch up later.

Another morning, Lampert checked the list of patients and noticed a telltale name: "Patient complaining of abdominal pain. Asking for hand lotion."

Frequent Flyer. "He was here five days ago," she said.

"Once in August. Once in July. Four times in June. Pretty much the same version of the complaint every time. Needs some hand lotion."

Another nurse said, "If you ask him to change into a gown, that sets him off and he walks out." Minus hand lotion.

Frequent Flyers who have no business in the emergency room are disturbing because they waste resources. An old nurse superstition is not to say aloud the name of a Frequent Flyer or they will surely return. Some of them, though, are simply sorry cases, refugees from life, the invisible people of the world that grip the hearts of the nurses.

Here came one now, a diminutive man with a chalky face, brought in by a paramedic who was on a chummy basis with him, given that he transported him virtually every week. The paramedic was a marathon runner, and the man bragged that he was his coach. The two had had a falling out some time ago but had patched things up. The paramedic mentioned how he was pleased to have gotten the man now, at the end of his shift, because he was an easy delivery, sure to be quick, and he had play tickets.

The man was undoubtedly the city's reigning Frequent Flyer champion. Not only was he a repeat presence at Lenox Hill but at pretty much all the city's ERs. He went to the ER like other people went to Starbucks. The paramedic said that he follows a calculated rotation, for some ERs grow weary of him and get nasty, then he gets nasty back. He was all smiles now as he acknowledged the nurses—hi, hi, good to see you again. He presented with shortness of breath, his default complaint, but his medical cause was really shortness of love. He was lonely. Noticing his arrival, the assistant nurse manager on duty said: "He just needs a little love. He wants to say hello to his friends."

There had been others with bruising backstories of emptied lives that saddened the nurses. The guy who had been a millionaire, lost his wife in childbirth, fell apart as his fortune melted away and everything twisted out of control. He became homeless and a Frequent Flyer, grasping for a sense of belonging. Another enjoyed a well-cushioned life as a successful architect. His wife and kids were killed when they were hit by a drunk driver. Unmoored and no longer believing life held magic, he gravitated to an existence defined by idleness and alcohol. He drank himself to death.

The champion Frequent Flyer burst with charisma. He didn't demand much. The assistant nurse manager said, "He'll be up and out of here in ten minutes." Lampert said, "It's basically a social call."

The man gave Lampert a pleased greeting: "How you doing, Hadassah?"

"I'm doing fine, how are you?" she said.

"Oh, I'm not real good, but I'm hanging in there."

I went over and spoke to him. He said he had asthma and chronic obstructive pulmonary disease. He was sixty-one, retired from mid-level administrative work and lived in an SRO. "I move around the city a lot, checking things out, and wherever I happen to be, I go to the ER near there," he said. "I'll admit, I go a lot. A lot. Go figure. The day before, I was up in the Bronx and was at Montefiore. I was in Queens the other week and, wouldn't you know it, I needed the emergency room so I stopped at a few emergency rooms there. I'm what you call medical savvy, I know the places to go. Your health is all you got. You got to protect your health. How you doing?"

A sodden afternoon. A small, gleeful Asian man showed up. He spoke little English. He was seventy-six, with gray hair that expanded in many directions. He was incessantly happy, as if he didn't understand what this place was for. With the ER jam-packed, he was assigned a bed in front of the nurses' station. A woman in a dreamy state was in a bed next to him and was as close to his bed as was possible without overlapping it. People streamed past, including a man carrying a urine sample and a woman beating the air with her arms and mumbling: "If I ever get out of here alive, I'm moving to Finland."

In order to communicate with the high-spirited man, Lampert wheeled over a video translation device that connected her with a translator who spoke Mandarin, the man's language. The compact man had been there just the other day, his complaint being that he had taken his blood pressure at home and it was somewhat high. It was his pattern of behavior. Check his blood pressure. A smidgeon high. On to the ER.

Using the translator, Lampert questioned him. The basic outline of his story had the same arc as a few days ago. His home reading was high. Get to the ER.

The man was hard of hearing, and he did not speak his answers. He shouted them, as if trying to be heard over roadwork. The whole ER could hear him. You could hear him in Queens.

He listened intently to each question, craning one ear toward the video screen, before detonating his answers. Lampert tried to have him lower the volume. She was having no success.

Shhh.

Shouting.

Shhh.

Shouting.

Shhh.

Shouting.

A doctor unavoidably eavesdropping on the amplified exchanges pivoted from what he was doing and said to Lampert: "Tell him I'm going to break his blood pressure machine."

Another doctor contributed: "Tell him his blood pressure is elevated because he's shouting."

Under continued questioning from Lampert, who was having trouble repressing her laughter, he shouted that he took medication for his blood pressure, but the prescription had expired, he didn't know why, didn't know why his cardiologist hadn't intervened. After conferring with a doctor, Lampert told him they would renew his prescription here but go see the cardiologist soon.

Within twenty minutes, Lampert discharged him. Her discharge instructions were to visit CVS, fill his prescription, and soften his allegiance to the blood pressure machine. He high-fived Lampert and departed merrily for CVS.

Besides the patient not in need of care, there is also the opposite, the patient rejecting necessary care. On this same day, Lampert experienced that as well.

The woman was in her seventies, with a wispy frame. She had abdominal pain. A doctor told her that she needed to have a CAT scan. In an unemotive voice, she said she didn't want it. A friend was with her and she didn't like the woman's recalcitrance. The doctor told her that he was a "go-home doctor," that if something didn't seem absolutely necessary to him, he always advised don't do it, go home. But he definitely felt this was not a go-home matter. After observing her brushing off the doctor for a third time—with him telling her, "It's up to you. It's your body"—her friend took to the offense. Wagging her finger in the woman's face, she said, "I will not talk to you anymore if you don't do this. I will not be your friend anymore. I am not kidding. I will not talk to you, believe me."

The woman remained resistant.

Her friend said, "Do you want to die a terrible death? Is that what you want? That is awful, that is torture. You do not want to die that death. I'm going out to get something to eat."

She went over to Lampert and told her, "I'm going to get something. She is just so stubborn. I had to threaten her with ending our friendship."

Lampert said, "Yes, she needs that. But it will have to be her decision."

The friend returned for one more exchange with the woman: "I love you. But you don't love me if you don't do this."

"I do love you," the woman said. "I don't want to do this."

"Okay, go home. Go home. Do what you want. I can do what I want."

Then she hugged her and gave her a kiss.

Nurses and doctors give their best professional advice. But they can't compel a patient to follow it. Their bodies, their lives, their choices.

Once the woman's friend had departed, I went to speak to her to learn her reasoning. Not long ago, she had been at the hospital to be treated for pancreatitis and had had some gall-stones removed. Three days ago, she was experiencing stom-ach pains and went to an ambulatory care center, where she had a CAT scan. Nothing showed up. She felt better, went home. Then pain again, and so she came here. She saw no reason to repeat the rigamarole of a CAT scan just three days after the last one.

Mulling it over, though, she said she was going to tell the doctor to do it. "My friend said she wouldn't be my friend anymore. She threatened me and she meant it. I don't want to lose her. I'll do it."

In this instance, a devoted friend made the difference. Didn't always happen. Lampert was gratified to see that this time it did.

17

One day seven people came to the emergency room wanting to kill themselves. It was a bad number, a miserable number. This disquieting string didn't strike Lampert as remarkable. Suicidal people regularly arrived at the ER to be made to want to live again. Sometimes they piled up. It was hard to figure. Had sad, hopeless thoughts infiltrated everyone in New York? "It happens," Lampert said. "Unfortunate, but it happens."

The charge nurse gave one of them to Lampert. It was a young, gawky woman with gleaming hair. Her distraught parents had brought her in. Lampert spoke to her gently. The woman sat stoically and kept examining her hands, as if they held answers. Trapped, she told Lampert that she simply wished to die, couldn't stand herself, that she had been unraveling for four years, was on and off her medication. Lampert reassured her that they were here for her. She took blood. It was necessary to medically clear her, then a pysch consult arrived to decide on what to do next. It was his decision to admit her to the psych ward.

The psychiatrist came over to Lampert to advise her of the resolution. He said she told him she didn't want to "be with the crazies." He told her it was inaccurate to think of the population that way, that there was another young woman just like her up there. She felt reassured.

One of the other nurses asked him about the psych ward, she had never been there. "It looks like any other ward, except there are bars on the windows," he said. He said there weren't too many patients there walking around like zombies, but mentioned that he did get attacked once by "someone really far gone."

"Oh wow," Lampert said.

"Then I came down here with an ice pack on my forehead."

Now another one. A teenager, college student. She came in by ambulance with her psychiatrist. The psychiatrist had called the ambulance when she found that the young woman had written a note saying she planned to kill herself by jumping off the Brooklyn Bridge by Wednesday. This was Monday. She had been having suicidal thoughts for years, had once sliced herself with a razor.

She wore glasses and torn jeans, and carried her sorrow on her face. Lampert pulled up a chair, patted her on the shoulder, gave her a big smile, and asked her if she felt safe there. She said she did. She said, "I'm going to cry."

"Cry," Lampert said. "Maybe I'll cry, too." The young woman smiled and almost laughed.

Suicidal patients are delicate encounters. You tiptoe into their life. "You have to be very respectful," Lampert told me. "You don't want to pry too much. But you have to make sure there's no active plan. You have to make sure they feel safe. I talk quietly and gently. You don't stand over them. I always get a chair and sit next to them. I don't want to seem that I'm overbearing. To me, sitting down next to them is the most important thing. A lot of nurses don't do it. I do. There have been studies done that show patients have more satisfaction and feel safer and more trusting when a nurse or doctor is sitting rather than standing. When you're standing, it's like you're ready to leave. When you're sitting, you're saying, I'm here to listen. We had a whole workshop on how to interact with a patient and how to do things in a humanistic way. Sitting was one of the key things. Also, explaining things without jargon. Treating the patient like a person and not a dog. Body language is a very big thing."

Now Lampert asked the young woman a bit about the circumstances, but not much. She didn't want to dwell on what had brought her here and set her off. A psych consult would be asking her anyway. She had the young woman smiling, laughing some more. It was something. She took blood to medically clear her. Later, it would be decided to transfer her to another psychiatric facility for treatment.

———

Nurses' station chatter:

"I had a really good meatball salad yesterday."

"She's trying to get a tax write-off because she washes her scrubs."

"Everyone's making fun of me and talking like they've got money growing on trees. Let me in your backyard."

"Upgrade for an AFib."

"I'm flipping bed eight."

"Need anything?"

"A bottle of wine."

"What color wine? Red? White? Rosé?"

"I guess red. There's a little chill in the air."

"Do you remember the first IV you did?"

"Yeah, I did it on you."

"Did you get it?"

"Not even close."

"I used to practice on my little brother."

"What?"

"You know when you're so exhausted, you're running on cortisol levels? That's me. I'm a little grouchy. Normally, I'm a very nice person."

"Don't bother me. Today is Don't Bother Luisa Day."

"Okay, I'll bother you tomorrow."

"You know how bad a grandma I'm going to be? I'm going

to give them everything they want. I'm probably going to give them diabetes, because I'm going to give them every candy they want, every candy made."

"I'm in a really bad mood, but I'm happy."

"I want to give this guy the Malocchio—if you're wondering, that's the Italian evil eye."

"I was watching football last night, the Packers and the Cowboys, and my son says, 'There's a team named the Cowboys?' and I'm like, what? That's not my kid. Not my kid. I need a new kid."

"Did you hear that someone stole a heart monitor at NYU? An eighteen-year-old. He just took it off the wall and put it in his backpack and walked out. What's he going to do with a heart monitor?"

"Maybe his father is a doctor and starting a clinic."

"Maybe he really, really likes heart monitors."

"I'm getting ready to eat myself to oblivion."

The front walk-in triage nurse was swamped, so Lampert went to assist with the scurry of arrivals.

Young, gangling woman with butter-colored hair and a raspy voice. Had had a migraine every day since June. This was mid-September. But never as bad as now. Medicine hadn't helped.

Lampert's expression softened, and she said, "I suffer from migraines, so I feel your pain."

The woman's eyes clouded. She smiled. "Thank you for that."

Hulking man with swollen left elbow.

"Do you have pain?"

"No. But I don't like the looks of it."

"Have you been outside?"

"I'm always outside. I'm a doorman."

"Oh, but not in the woods. You're in the jungle."

Next, pencil-thin young woman with back pain. Took muscle relaxant at five a.m. because she couldn't sleep. No help. Now felt hot everywhere. In she went.

And: Woman hurt her left foot at work at two p.m., three hours ago. A metal bench fell on it. "I can't even move this foot up and down. It hurts." Pain level 8½.

Next: Older woman with chest pain for three days. "It's inside, so if you touch me you won't find it. It travels when I move."

Next: Young, buffed-up man tripped and fell on the subway. Right leg hurt. Limping. Happened twenty minutes ago. "It's like it's going to fall off."

Lampert said, "Don't worry, it won't fall off. We will make sure your leg won't fall off."

Guy was in Puerto Rico over the weekend, in the ocean,

got flipped over by waves, thinks he broke something. Was on crutches he bought in Puerto Rico. Though no expert, he said he got a good price for crutches in Puerto Rico.

Bald guy, who said, "There's screaming pain in my chest and my whole head is pounding. It feels as if my whole chest is going to explode."

"Have you taken any drugs?" Lampert asked.

"I took a couple of Mollys."

"Have you been drinking?"

"I drank two Coronas about three hours ago."

That would have been at six-thirty in the morning. Level 2.

Teenage boy with parents. Bonked his head on the bunk bed. His mom: "He's grown too tall. We've got to get rid of that top bunk."

Lampert agreed that a bunk bed replacement would be a good prescription.

Guy with abdominal discomfort: "It's not really pain, it's discomfort."

Lampert asked: "What did you eat last night?"

"Actually, it was takeout. Domino's. Do you think maybe I need to switch pizza places?"

18

It was late afternoon. A sharp, blue day. The emergency room was its usual hubbub of activity, dizzy with maladies. The nurses fanned out, encumbered with tasks, scattering in service to their patients. After spending many hours here in the trenches of medical care, so different from outside in the world, I found a certain mesmerism, almost a hypnotism, to the ephemerality of the pulsating arrivals, the hanging, one after the other, of the clear IV bags, the blood draws, the delivery of medicine, the nurses so busy with their ac- knowledged mission of preserving life. They were needed everywhere, answering lights, answering moans. One nurse described "being dragged around like a mop."

Lampert commiserated. Other nurses commiserated, in a feedback loop common in the ER. You got emotional support from other nurses and gave it back. Who else could under- stand the lives they led? The grand beauty of what they did. How hard it was. To do this work well, you had to give self- lessly all the time to the needs of strangers. You squeezed in time for your own thoughts, even to fulfill your hunger. Juggling six patients, her time no longer pliant, Lampert, desperate for food, ordered a bagel online to be delivered to the ER. It came after a leisurely interlude, the provider clearly not recognizing the request of a bagel as an emergency.

But the busyness was speaking to her. At this particular time on this particular day, this was her place, her room.

Lampert took information from a woman, her face runneled with lines, apparently suffering from alcohol withdrawal. Lampert asked her if she took drugs. Discomforted by the question, she winced and said, "Not lately."

"What's not lately?"

"Well, marijuana a day ago. Cocaine a week ago."

Next, Lampert gave medication to another woman, who mentioned she would be leaving soon on a trip.

"Where are you going?" Lampert asked.

"London."

"Oh, to see the queen."

"Yeah, sure."

"To have tea with the queen."

"Oh please," the woman said.

A young man with good posture arrived on a stretcher in his pajamas. The ever-alert Lampert glanced at him and said, "Hey, pajama party."

She saw to a one-legged man having chest pains. About to

give him medication, she asked his birthday and he said it was February 14. Lampert said, "That's a great birthday. Everyone should have that birthday. That's love day."

Shuttled back behind a computer, working on the chart of another patient, Lampert, feeling mildly mutinous, said to a doctor seated near her, "Abdominal pain workup is the worst thing on the planet. Labs. Blood. Imaging. Pain medication . . ."

The doctor said, "That's like saying I hate when the sun comes up."

One of the other nurses arrived with a bag of assorted candy. Lampert's eyes widened. Snacks, especially chocolate, always an important moment in the ER, enlivening any shift.

Lampert said, "Can I have an Almond Joy? I love Almond Joy. It's for my sanity."

An eavesdropping doctor said, "Who chooses Almond Joy?"

Lampert said, "It's coconut and almond and chocolate, works for me."

The doctor said, "I'm more a Snickers man."

The woman in bed 3 and her accompanying husband were jabbing back and forth. She complained that she had wanted soup, tomato or chicken. The husband said, "They didn't have soup." He took a large bite out of his pastrami sandwich. The wife said, "I wanted soup." The husband said, "I said they didn't have no soup." The wife said, "I need soup." The tormented husband said, "Hrumphh." The wife, her eyes livid, said, "Do you know what I'd like to do to you this very minute?"

Lampert and the other nurses gave each other knowing looks. Rolled their eyes.

Lampert drifted past the curtained, transitional spaces bursting with patients. A seventy-four-year-old woman with a tinny voice and ghostly appearance arrived from a nursing home. There was a lot wrong with her. Fever yesterday. Unresponsive today. Hypertension. Diabetes. Pacemaker. There was anguish on her crumpled face.

Their eyes locked. "Hi, I'm Hadassah, I'm a nurse here and I'm going to take care of you."

No recognizable response, just some sighs.

With practiced ease, Lampert took her vitals, put in a line, hung an IV bag, took blood, connected her to a heart monitor—the ER drill.

"You okay, honey, what's going on?"

"I don't know. I think I'm sick."

"You have an infection. Your blood pressure is low. We're going to take care of you."

She delicately put her stethoscope to the woman's skin and listened with concern to her lungs. "Very noisy. How long did you have this cough?"

"I don't know. I don't know much of anything."

"We have to get a urine sample. I'm going to put a catheter into your bladder."

She moaned. Lampert squeezed her hand. "What's the matter, honey?"

"I feel . . ."

"What do you feel?"

"I feel something's wrong."

"You have an infection. We're going to take care of you. I'm going to clean out your mouth. Your mouth is very dry. And we're giving you antibiotics for pneumonia."

"I'm scared."

"Don't be scared. We're giving you medicine for the cough. I don't want you to be scared."

"Okay, give me the medicine. But why all these wires?"

"We're making you better."

"Believe me, I don't know what's going on."

"What's the matter? Do you know where we are? Where are we? Tell me where we are."

"I don't know."

"You do know. Are we in your home? Where are we? We're in Lenox Hill Hospital."

"Lenox Hill Hospital."

"What year is it?"

"I don't know."

"It's 2019. Who's the president? Tell me who the president is. Donald. What's the last name?"

She rocked her head to the side, and said, "I'm scared."

"I know. You keep telling me you're scared. Who's the president?"

"I'm scared."

As Lampert swiveled to do her charting on a nearby computer, she kept talking to the woman, trying to rally her hopes, the fading promise of her life. She had a bad infection of her leg, possible pneumonia, who knew what else, a complex of enemies. A doctor came to see her, looked the woman over, consulted with Lampert and said she would have someone from Intensive Care come by, decide if she needed to be admitted there. She was taken for a CAT scan, then brought back. The doctor departed. It was the woman and Lampert, patient and nurse.

Outside, the city darkened. The fast-paced emergency room, as it inevitably did, was getting overcrammed, always in constant demand. The noise level was up, rushed, urgent tones. The crackle of announcements. This woman, sickness sinking through her, would later move up to Intensive Care. Lampert would say goodbye to her and not see her again, or know whether her life would resume in a recognizable form. New patients with their own private emergencies would replace her.

Now the woman said, "I don't know what's going on. I really don't."

Lampert told her, "It's okay, honey. You don't need to know. We need to know."

"I'm so uncomfortable, just so uncomfortable."

"You're uncomfortable. What would make you comfortable?"

The woman reached out her hand. Lampert took it.

She regarded the woman staring at her kind eyes in wonderment. "It's okay," Lampert said. "We've got you. I've got you. I'm going to take care of you. That's what we do. We take care of people."

Life and death, every day in the emergency room. It always came down to this, at the bedside.

The woman, lying motionless in the flood of light, gave a partial, crooked smile. Lampert released her hand and its fragile bones and patted her head. She looked closely at her. She returned to the computer and resumed her charting. Time passed. Over her shoulder, she said, "We're here. I'm here. I'm always here."

ACKNOWLEDGMENTS

Thanks to Stuart Roberts, senior editor at Simon & Schuster, for inviting me to undertake this project and for shepherding it to publication. Thanks, as well, to Emily Simonson for her editing prowess.

No book of this sort is possible without full access to its subject. I'm indebted to Lenox Hill Hospital for embracing the idea and affording me unrestricted access to its emergency room. In particular, I'd like to thank Irene Macyk, Cathy Fogarty, Dr. Yves Duroseau, and Barbara Osborn for their good-spirited help, as well as all the patients I observed and the many members of the ER who tolerated my presence while they did their important work.

Above all, I want to express my gratitude to Hadassah Lampert, a truly exceptional nurse, for generously allowing me to spend many shifts alongside her in the ER, teaching me firsthand what it means to be a nurse.

I'm grateful to my agent, Andrew Blauner, who brought

this series to my attention and has been such a devoted advocate.

Finally, as always, thanks to my wife, Susan Saiter Sullivan, and my daughter, Samantha, for their everlasting support and for being there.

APPENDIX

NURSING ASSOCIATIONS

American Nurses Association (ANA). Founded in 1896, this is one of the principal associations of registered nurses. It provides educational opportunities and acts as an advocate for nurses.

https://www.nursingworld.org/

Emergency Nurses Association (ENA). This is the leading organization representing emergency room nurses, counting forty thousand members. It advocates for excellence in emergency care and offers educational resources.

https://www.ena.org/

National Nurses United (NNU). This is one of the largest unions and professional associations for registered nurses, and a central voice in calling for better conditions for nurses and patients.

https://www.nationalnursesunited.org/

The American Association of Colleges of Nursing (AACN). Representing more than eight hundred nursing schools, the AACN serves as a voice for academic nursing.

https://www.aacnnursing.org/

INFORMATION ON LICENSING

National Council of State Boards of Nursing (NCSBN). This organization of the state nursing regulatory bodies offers information on the licensure and certification exams nurses are required to take and how to register for them and what to expect.

https://www.ncsbn.org/nclex.htm

MEDICAL RESOURCES

Medscape. A popular online resource for drug and disease information and medical news.

https://www.medscape.com/

UpToDate. A subscription online resource for medical information used by many clinicians.

https://www.uptodate.com/home

ADDITIONAL READING

Notes on Nursing: What It Is, and What It Is Not (1859)
by Florence Nightingale

A brief and clear-eyed advice book on the nature of nursing, which is remarkably relevant even today, by the founder of modern nursing.

Nurse: The True Story of Mary Benjamin, R.N. (1978)
by Peggy Anderson

A vivid, fascinating account, written in the first person, of eight weeks in the life of a nurse on the medicine floors of a pseudonymous large urban hospital.

The Shift: One Nurse, Twelve Hours, Four Patients' Lives (2016)
by Theresa Brown

A detailed, expertly written recounting of a single shift in the cancer ward of a Pittsburgh hospital by a nurse and *New York Times* contributor.

Critical Care: A New Nurse Faces Death, Life, and Everything in Between (2011)
by Theresa Brown

A poignant memoir of an oncology nurse's first year on the job.

A Nurse's Story: Life, Death, and In-Between in an Intensive Care Unit (2004)
by Tilda Shalof

A very well-done rendering by a nurse of what it's like working in the intensive care unit of a Canadian hospital.

I Wasn't Strong Like This When I Started Out: True Stories of Becoming a Nurse (2013)
edited by Lee Gutkind

A superb collection of the reflections of nurses on pivotal moments from the job, by a diverse array of nurses at varying stages in their careers.

Sheehy's Emergency Nursing: Principles and Practices
(7th Edition, 2019)
edited by Vicki Sweet and Andi Foley

A comprehensive review of the basic procedures and issues of emergency nursing written by emergency room nurses.

Fast Facts for the ER Nurse: Emergency Room Orientation in a Nutshell (2013)
by Jennifer R. Buettner

Excellent orientation guide, with succinct chapters on how to address key disorders that appear repeatedly in the ER.

Mosby's Pharmacology Memory NoteCards: Visual, Mnemonic, and Memory Aids for Nurses (5th Edition, 2019)

A highly functional collection of cards for nursing students to learn drugs and pharmacology topics, using illustrations, humor and mnemonics, among other learning aids.

Becoming Nursey: From Code Blues to Code Browns, How to Care for Patients and Yourself (2019)
by Kati Kleber

An informative, readable exploration by a critical care nurse on how to become a caring nurse while also caring for yourself.